Kids Lunch Boxes

**101 Tasty, Fresh, Fun and Healthy
School Lunchbox Ideas and Recipes
Your Kids Will Love To Eat!**

TABLE OF CONTENTS

PART I: SAVORY

PART II: SWEET

DISCLAIMER

The author has taken every care to ensure that any recipes that contain food which could spoil or turn bad over the course of a day, such as meat, fish, or egg, are clearly identified in the directions, as requiring additional attention in regards to packaging the food.

In these instances, the author has made suggestions in relation to keeping the food at a suitable temperature, such as with cold packs and insulated lunch boxes, and/or by storing in a refrigerator before consumption.

The author and publisher would ask, that as a matter of due care, that in addition to these suggestions, you exercise your own common sense here as to what is an appropriate level of due diligence when packaging and transporting any food items, including the recipes herein.

And as such, the author and publisher of this book takes no responsibility or accepts any liability for improper packaging or storage of food products, or misuse in preparation of ingredients in any way.

Now that we have that disclaimer behind us, let's get to the cooking!

FOREWORD

Hello, my fellow lover of lunchbox variety!

My name is Naomi Potter and I just love to create healthy choices that are exciting and interesting experiences for my kids to munch on during lunch.

Oh, the joys of school! Everyone remembers those days. Hours spent at a desk pouring over subjects, with the occasional furtive glance at the clock in an attempt to make the boring bits go faster.

Let's be honest, as interesting as Equivalent Fractions and Shakespeare can be, that isn't necessarily what our kids look forward to all day.

Yet there's one shining beacon of scrumptious freedom that awaits!

A beautiful moment that hasn't changed all that much since we ourselves were staring at the blackboard.

Lunch!

This bastion of time is guaranteed, right from your child's first day of kindergarten all the way through to their graduation day.

It's a period of nutritious re-energy, preparing us for that upcoming afternoon of Math or Science, as well as being a revered period of socialization, laughter and play.

Throughout history, people have always bonded together around food and it's clear that kids are no different. As such, giving your children the best possible meal to compliment this very important time of day is paramount.

As is often the case, managing to find the time to balance preparing a healthy lunch during the chaos of the usual morning rush, however, is decidedly not easy.

In an increasingly hectic world the five to ten minutes set aside to throw something in a lunch box could be the difference between forgetting to get them wearing the right gear for a sports day, or heaven forbid, neglecting to pack their possibly already overdue assignment.

Often times, quickly forking over some lunch money to use at the cafeteria, seems like the easiest option.

The problem, of course, is that school food is rarely that healthy. Greasy burgers slathered in ketchup, deep fried tater tots and nary a green bean in sight.

It's not rocket science to realize that those sorts of nutrient lacking foods are not what kids need to get them through the rest of their day.

Kids are constantly changing. They get taller, bigger, faster... and naturally, their food choices need to reflect this unique period of growth.

What we feed our children can surely affect their health, wellness, and eating habits for years to come.

But how can we do this? How do we create nutritious and delicious meals our kids will actually *love* to eat? It's easy!

With a little preparation, some free time on the weekend or the night before, and a freezer or refrigerator close by, you can have a horde of healthy, yummy foods on standby ready for the lunchbox.

These 101 savory and sweet recipe suggestions, offer everything a lunch box could need, gobble down treats, crunchy snacks and mouthwatering main courses, all easy to store and transport to school, and full of goodness.

They are also great fun to make while bonding with your kids, stirring batter in bowls, mashing down the mixture for cookies, and adding exciting toppings to mini homemade healthy pizza bites.

And all the while, they'll be learning healthy eating habits and enjoying eating creations they helped make with their own hands.

So take back control of the playground lunch! Reclaim the morning rush! Give these delectable recipes a try!

You'll be so glad you did.

Naomi Potter

PART I: SAVORY

ANYTHING GOES POCKETS

This is a great food for leftovers because literally anything can be put into it.

Makes 14

INGREDIENTS:

14 egg roll wraps

1 can kidney beans, drained and rinsed

1 cup cheese, shredded

1 bell pepper, seeds removed and finely chopped

½ cup Greek yogurt

½ cup pasta sauce

1 onion, finely chopped

1 clove of garlic, finely minced

Coconut oil (for frying)

Water

DIRECTIONS:

1. In a small frying pan, melt the oil.

2. Add in the garlic, beans, onion and pepper.

3. Cook until the vegetables are soft. Your house will smell amazing and don't be surprised if people are drawn by the smell of garlic.

4. Once the vegetables are cooked add them to a medium bowl.

5. Pour your pasta sauce on top of the bean mixture and stir to mix and coat everything.

6. Lay a wonton wrapper on a cutting board. Be careful not to get it wet.

7. Then take the Greek yogurt and spread it over the wrapper, making sure to leave about a centimeter around the edge (or the width of the tip of your index finger).

8. Spoon about 2-3 tablespoons worth of mixture onto the Greek yogurt and sprinkle with cheese.

9. Dip your finger in water and run it along the edge of the wrapper and fold it over, closing it firmly.

10. Repeat this with remaining ingredients.

11. Reheat the frying pan and melt approximately ¼ cup coconut oil

12. Once the oil is hot place the pockets one at a time into the hot oil.

13. Cook until crispy and golden brown and then flip over.

14. If eating immediately, leave to cool for 5 – 10 minutes before serving.

15. Or refrigerate overnight and ensure that the pockets are well wrapped the next day and placed in an insulated lunch box.

16. Use a freezer pack to keep the food cool – especially if you add meat to the mix.

BACON AND EGG BEFORE SCHOOL MUFFINS

A compact version of a breakfast and brunch favorite, this muffin is a delicious, before school breakfast meal that kids and adults will love.

Makes 10 servings

INGREDIENTS:

1 can refrigerator biscuits

4 eggs

4 tbsp milk

5 slices of bacon, cooked and crumbled.

Cheese, shredded

Salt and pepper to taste

DIRECTIONS:

1. Preheat oven to 400°F and grease a muffin tin with no-stick spray or butter.

2. Separate the biscuit dough and roll out each biscuit until it is just a little bit larger than the muffin pans.

3. Press flattened dough into each muffin hole, making sure to press down all the way.

4. Whisk together eggs, milk, salt and pepper.

5. Then pour the egg mixture over the biscuits, filling only half-way, and sprinkle with cheese and bacon.

6. Be sure you do not overfill or else you may end up with a horrible mess.

7. Bake in the oven for 10-12 minutes or until the eggs are set.

8. Remove from the pan and serve immediately.

9. If there are any left to send to school ensure that the muffins are well wrapped and placed an insulated lunch box.

10. If possible, store in a school refrigerator before eating.

BACON BIRD SANDWICH

For bird fans, or Angry Bird fans, this little sandwich is sure to please. Easy to assemble and to send in a lunchbox it will be a pleasant surprise for your littlest fans.

Makes 1 serving

INGREDIENTS:

1 slice whole wheat bread

1 slice white bread

2 tomato slices

2 slices bacon, cooked

2 tbsp Greek yogurt

2 Cheese discs

2 green peas

1 carrot disc, cut in half

2 grape tomatoes

1 tbsp cream cheese

Bean sprouts

DIRECTIONS:

1. On a plate, place the two piece of bread on top of each other and carefully cut out one large circle out of both pieces and save those and two 1" pieces of crust.

2. Throw away the excess or have your little ones feed it to the birds.

3. On the whole wheat disc spread the Greek yogurt and lay on the tomato slices and cooked bacon.

4. Then, take the white piece and cut a wide crescent moon shape out of one side.

5. Keep both pieces; this will be your mouth.

6. Lay the pieces on top of the tomato.

7. Using the cream cheese, stick the crusts on the top in the shape of eyebrows.

8. Beneath that, place the small cheese circles with the peas on top of that (these can also both be affixed with cream cheese if desired).

9. For the beak, lay the carrot halves along the crescent moon.

10. Then lay the sandwich on top of a pie of bean sprouts and place two grape tomatoes at the bottom to serve as the feet.

11. Send to school in an insulated lunch box or one with a freezer pack to keep cool.

12. You could use a drink bottle for this – freeze full of juice overnight! This will save you even more time in the morning.

13. If possible, store in a school refrigerator before eating.

BAKED SWEET CORN AND CHICKEN TACOS

Offering a good combination of sweet and spicy, this lunch is perfect for a cool fall or winter day.

Makes 4 servings

INGREDIENTS:

4 oz cherry tomatoes, washed and quartered.

4 oz whole kernel corn, frozen or canned

2 green onions, finely sliced.

2 oz fresh or frozen spinach

4 large whole wheat or corn tortillas

12 oz pulled barbecue chicken

1 cup grated cheese

2 tbsp sweet chili sauce (optional)

Grated cheese for topping (optional)

DIRECTIONS:

1. Preheat oven to 350°F.

2. In a bowl, mix together vegetables, tomato and sauce (if using) and set aside.

3. Lay the wraps out and lay the chicken and cheese on it, topping with the tomato mixture and leaving 1" around the edge.

4. Roll up and lay in a greased baking sheet, seam side down. If desire, sprinkle with grated cheese.

5. Cook 10-15 minutes or until tops are slightly

6. Can be served immediately.

7. To transport, wrap in foil and place in a lidded container. As this recipe has chicken in it, it is important to keep it cool until lunch time.

8. Remember to add a freezer pack and store in a fridge if you can.

BAKED SWEET POTATO OMELET

Omelets are a delicious and popular food however they are not very easy to transport. This recipe combines the best parts of an omelet in an easily transportable manner.

Makes 4 servings

INGREDIENTS:

15 oz potatoes, peeled and sliced into thick rounds

15 oz sweet potatoes, peeled and sliced into thick rounds

1 tbsp butter

1 tbsp olive oil

1 leek, white part only, sliced

1 garlic clove, crushed

½ cup cream

6 eggs, lightly beaten

Salt and pepper

¼ cup grated parmesan

DIRECTIONS:

1. Preheat oven to 350°F.

2. Line two baking sheet with tinfoil and spray with nonstick spray.

3. Place the potatoes on the trays and cook for 15 minutes or until they are soft.

4. While this is happening, heat a frying pan and melt some butter in it.

5. Put in the leeks and cook until they are soft then add the garlic and cook for another minute or two.

6. Lay potato slices on top of the leak mixture, alternating between regular potato and sweet potato, until they are all placed.

7. Combine the cream and eggs with the seasonings, whisking to mix.

8. Pour it into the frying pan and cook for 10-15 minute or until the eggs are almost set.

9. Heat griddle to medium and place the omelet on it, sprinkling with cheese.

10. Cook until the eggs are completely set and the edges are golden brown.

11. Serve immediately or put the omelet on a plate and cover.

12. It will last approximately 3 days in the refrigerator.

13. Send to school in an insulated lunch box or one with a freezer pack to keep cool.

14. Add finger a salad of some tomatoes, cucumber strips, bell peppers and perhaps a green spring onion or two!

15. If it is possible store in a school refrigerator until eaten.

BLACK FRIDAY SANDWICH

Thanksgiving, Christmas, Easter...whatever holiday you are talking about, turkey and cranberry sauce often play a primary role and there are always leftovers. This sandwich is a creative twist on a turkey sandwich that allows you to use up those holiday extras.

Makes 10 servings

INGREDIENTS:

20 oz turkey breast, sliced

½ cup cranberry sauce

10 cheese slices

½ head lettuce, shredded

20 slices whole wheat bread

DIRECTIONS:

1. Lay bread on a plate or the counter.

2. On one slice, spread a layer of cranberry sauce to desired thickness.

3. Then top with turkey breast, cheese and lettuce.

4. Finally, top with the second piece of bread

5. Can be served whole or cut in half.

6. Wrap carefully in foil or plastic wrap and place in a rigid container to send to school.

7. Remember to use an insulated lunch box or one with a freezer pack to keep cool.

8. If possible, store in a school refrigerator before eating.

9. It is a good idea not to send too much lunch so there are no warm leftovers to be munched on later as this could be a health hazard in warm weather.

BREAD WRAPPED PIZZA STUFFERS

Easy to make and easy to pack, this recipe is a neat solution for packing pizza for your children's' lunch.

Makes 16 pieces or 2 large logs

INGREDIENTS:

½ baguette

8 oz cherry tomatoes

1 tbsp olive oil

1 tsp salt and pepper

1 tsp oregano

2 tbsp tomato paste

½ cup cooked and diced bacon or ham (optional)

½ cup mozzarella cheese

DIRECTIONS:

1. Preheat oven to 400°F.

2. Line a baking sheet with tin foil and grease if desired.

3. Add the tomatoes, spices and oil to a medium bowl and mix until the tomatoes are entirely covered in oil and the spices are evenly distributed.

4. Place on tray and cook for 15 minutes or until the tomatoes blister.

5. They will look slightly brown and a little dehydrated.

6. At this point, remove them from the oven and allow them to cool.

7. Using your hands or a small fork, press the tomatoes until they form a watery paste.

8. If you like you can remove the skins at this point but it is not necessary.

9.   Cut the baguette in half and rip out the soft part.

10. Spread the tomato paste on the now empty crust and, if desired, sprinkle with cheese or spices.

11. Spoon in some of the tomato mixture and add on bacon bits and cheese.

12. Place on a lined baking tray and cook at 350°F for 15 minutes.

13. Cut into portions to serve.

14. Refrigerate overnight if you are going to use these as part of a school lunch box.

15. Send to school in an insulated lunch box or one with a freezer pack to keep cool, and if possible, store in a school refrigerator before eating.

CARNIVAL CHICKEN SANDWICH

With a wonderful helping of protein and a dose of vitamin C, this sandwich is more than your average lunch.

Makes 7 sandwiches

INGREDIENTS:

$1/_3$ cup Greek yogurt

2 tbsp lemon juice

24 oz cups barbecued chicken meat, chopped

2 tbsp roasted walnuts, roughly chopped

¼ cup fresh tarragon, roughly chopped

1 cup red and green grapes, halved

¼ cup dried cranberries

14 plain bread sliced, whole wheat preferred

DIRECTIONS:

1. Whisk together sour cream, lemon juice and a little bit of seasoning in a small bowl.

2. In a separate bowl, mix together chicken, walnuts, tarragon, three quarters of the grape halves and the cranberries.

3. Combine the cream mixture with the chicken mixture gently and divide evenly among seven pieces of the bread.

4. Top with remaining slices of bread and then garnish with remaining grape halves.

5. When serving, cut into halves diagonally or leave whole.

6. If you are going to use this sandwich for a school lunch ensure that it is cool and kept cool until eaten. An insulated lunch box would be ideal for this.

CHEESY BEEF RICE BAKE

A great alternative to hamburger helper and mac and cheese, this cheesy meal is sure to please even the pickiest eater!

Makes 6-8 servings

INGREDIENTS:

3 cups cooked rice

$1/3$ cup parmesan cheese, grated

4 eggs, lightly beaten

½ tsp paprika

1 cup cheddar cheese, grated

2 tbsp olive oil

1 onion, diced

2 cloves of garlic, crushed

1 lb ground beef

2 tbsp tomato paste

1 can tomatoes, diced

1 tsp beef stock

1 cup water

1 ½ cup mixed vegetables, frozen

DIRECTIONS:

1. Preheat oven to 350°F.

2. Line a cake pan with foil and grease with either butter or non-stick spray. Set aside

3. Heat a frying pan over medium high heat and add the oil and garlic.

4. Cook until soft.

5. Add the ground beef and brown.

6. Stir in the tomato paste then the tomatoes, stock and water.

7. Stir thoroughly and bring to a boil.

8. Once at a boil, lower the heat and simmer for 15 minutes uncovered.

9. Add in the vegetables, stirring to distribute them, and lower the heat.

10. In a separate bowl combine the eggs, parmesan cheese and paprika.

11. Mix in the cook rice and pour into the prepared baking pan.

12. Pour the sauce over the rice and use a fork or spoon to mix all together.

13. Sprinkle with cheese and bake for 45 minutes.

14. If eating immediately, allow to cook for 10 minutes before cutting and serving.

15. For school, refrigerate overnight.

16. Place the beef and rice bake in rigid microwave proof container before you pack it for school and put it in an insulated lunch box.

17. Remember to include a spoon and fork for eating and a little note to your teacher to ask if they may re-heat the bake in the microwave.

18. Also ask if the bake may be kept in a fridge until break time!

CHEESY CHICKEN QUESADILLAS

Southwestern food is always popular but often unhealthy. This quesadilla, however, is both healthy and easy to pack in a lunch box.

Makes 8 wraps

INGREDIENTS:

8 tortillas (corn or flour)

6 tbsp cream cheese

3 shallots

2 cups cooked chicken, cubed

1 cup mozzarella

1 cup cheddar cheese

DIRECTIONS:

1. Place 4 tortillas face down on the counter.

2. In a small bowl, mix together the cream cheese and shallots then spread among the four tortillas.

3. Place a quarter of the chicken on each tortilla and top with cheese.

4. Then place one of the four remaining tortillas on top and press down gently.

5. Spray a frying pan with non-stick spray and heat over medium-high.

6. Place one quesadilla on the frying pan and cook until the bottom tortilla is slightly golden then flip and repeat.

7. The cheese should be nicely melted.

8. Cut in half with a pizza cutter or long knife and refrigerate overnight.

9. Send to school in a rigid container placed in a cool box.

10. If including salsa or chili sauce place it in a small sealed container so that it does not spill out.

11. Do ask your child's teacher if the lunch can be stored in a school refrigerator before eating.

CHEESY PIGS IN A BLANKET

Here's a delightful twist on an old favorite. Pigs in a blanket are an easy finger food that kids love and the cheese adds a slightly savory twist to the old classic.

Makes 12 servings

INGREDIENTS:

3 puff pastry sheets, defrosted

12 small sausages or hot dogs

Shredded cheddar cheese

1 egg, beaten

Marinara sauce, to serve

DIRECTIONS:

1. Preheat oven to 350°F.

2. Line a baking tray with tinfoil or parchment paper and grease with non-stick spray.

3. Cut defrosted puff pastry sheets into quarters. You should end up with 12 separate pieces.

4. Lay one sausage on the edge of the puff pastry quarter and sprinkle with cheddar cheese.

5. Slowly roll away from you, brushing the end edge with a little beaten egg to seal. At this point they can be frozen for up to one month.

6. If desired, brush tops of pastry with egg and then place in the oven for 30 minutes or until golden brown.

7. Refrigerate overnight.

8. Send to school with marinara sauce, in an insulated lunch box and if possible, store in a school refrigerator until lunchtime. Remember a napkin for sticky fingers!

CHICKEN CHILI PITA POCKET

*Whether you like a bit of sweetness or a bit of spice, this recipe is perfect.
It is easily transportable and perfect for packing in a lunch box.*

Make 2 servings

INGREDIENTS:

1 whole-wheat pita pocket

1 tbsp cream cheese

1 tsp sweet or spicy chili sauce

4 small lettuce leaves

½ cucumber, thinly grated or sliced

2 tbsp cooked chicken, shredded

1 tbsp carrot, coarsely grated

1 tbsp cheddar, coarsely grated

DIRECTIONS:

1. Slice pita in half to create two pockets and gently open each one to make the space inside easily accessible

2. In a bowl, combine cream cheese and chili sauce.

3. Spread over the inside of the pocket then layer half of the vegetables in each pocket.

4. Either serve immediately or refrigerate overnight.

5. The next morning place the pocket in a rigid container with a frozen juice bottle or freezer pack to keep it cool. Especially if the weather is hot!

6. It is important to keep chicken cold and refrigerated until eaten so permission to use the school refrigerator should be sort.

EGGS AND BACON QUICHE

This makes an excellent breakfast or brunch food. It's easy for smaller fingers to grasp but interesting enough that older kids and family members will look forward to seconds.

Makes 6 servings

INGREDIENTS:

1 sheet puff pastry

1 tbsp olive oil

1 onion, finely chopped

6 pieces of bacon, chopped

1 cup grated cheese

5 eggs

¾ cup heavy whipping cream

¾ cup milk

Salt and Pepper (optional)

DIRECTIONS:

1. Preheat oven to 350°F and defrost puff pastry according to box directions.

2. Grease a muffin tin with non-stick spray and set aside.

3. Cut the pastry into six equal sections using a knife or pizza cutter.

4. Lay one piece in each of the grease muffin holes, trimming any excess pastry from the edges.

5. In a frying pan, heat the oil and add the onion.

6. Add the bacon and cook until the bacon is crispy and the onions are transparent and aromatic.

7. Sprinkle the onion/bacon mixture evenly into each of the lined muffin holes.

8. In a small bowl, whisk the eggs with the cream, milk and seasonings.

9. Once thoroughly mixed, carefully pour on top of the bacon.

10. Bake 25 minutes or until the eggs are fully cooked and the pastry is puffy.

11. Refrigerate overnight.

12. Use an insulated lunch box to send the quiche to school as it is important to keep the meat and dairy products cool until eaten.

13. A rigid container with a frozen juice bottle placed next to the quiche would also work very well.

14. If liked a fresh salad would be a great accompaniment.

ENGLISH MUFFIN MINI PIZZAS

These mini pizzas are a healthy alternative to frozen pizza products and because of their small size they are easy to pack in a lunch box.

Makes 12 mini pizzas

INGREDIENTS:

1 package of 6 English muffins

1 jar tomato pizza sauce

1 medium tomato, thinly slices

2 tsp Italian herb seasoning.

1 green bell pepper, seeds removed and finely diced (optional)

3 pieces of bacon, cooked and crumbled

Shredded mozzarella cheese

DIRECTIONS:

1. Preheat oven to 350°F and line a baking sheet with foil. A toaster oven may also be used to make these.

2. Slice each muffin in half and place soft side up on the pan.

3. In a small bowl, mix together the pizza sauce and herbs.

4. Spread this liberally over each English muffin. On top of the paste, lay one thin tomato slice.

5. Sprinkle the pizzas with mozzarella cheese and add on the green pepper and bacon as a topping if desired.

6. Place in the oven or toaster oven and cook for 10-12 minutes or until cheese is melted and slightly golden.

7. Refrigerate overnight.

8. When packing the lunch in the morning remember to put in a freezer pack to keep the mini pizzas cool until eaten.

FIESTA BURRITOS

A tasty twist on a southwestern favorite, this is both easy to make and easy to store making it a snap for mid-week lunch.

Makes 24 burritos

INGREDIENTS:

1 onions, diced

25 oz minced chicken

2 cans of kidney beans, drained and mashed

1 ½ tbsp tomato paste

½ tsp mixed spice

½ tsp pepper

1 ½ tbsp vegetable broth

1 carrot, diced

1 green pepper, seeds removed and diced

½ cup salsa

1 cups shredded cheese

24 tortillas

DIRECTIONS:

1. Grease a frying pan with oil and sauté the onions until soft.
2. Add the chicken and brown, adding the carrots, tomato paste and peppers until they are also soft.
3. Put in seasonings, bullion and pepper then stir. Set aside and leave to cool slightly.
4. Lay out a square of tin foil in a pan and grease.
5. Lay a tortilla on the counter.

6. Spoon some salsa onto it and spread. If you aren't sure about having the salsa inside, you can use it as a topping instead.

7. After the salsa, add some of the chicken mixture into the burrito, sprinkle with cheese and fold over.

8. Repeat with remaining ingredients.

9. At this point you can wrap them in foil and freeze them. They keep for a month.

10. Top with a bit of salsa and cheese.

11. Place in oven for about 15 minutes at 350°F or until slightly toasted and the cheese is slightly melted.

12. Refrigerate overnight.

13. Pack the Burritos carefully the next morning in an insulated lunch box to keep it fresh especially as it contains minced chicken.

14. These can be eaten cold but it would be a good idea to ask your child's teacher to pop it in the microwave for a minute or so until heated completely through.

15. This is important because the chicken needs to be heated properly!

16. The Burritos could also be packed for school lunch straight from the freezer. It will defrost while waiting for lunch time.

17. Pack the cheese and sauce separately. They can be sprinkled on before or after the microwave heating.

FRENCH BREAD PIZZA

This pizza can be quickly put in the oven while preparing breakfast and packed into a lunchbox before the morning rush.

Makes 4 pizzas

INGREDIENTS:

1 French baguette

1 cup mozzarella cheese

2-8 oz can tomato paste

5-oz cherry tomatoes, halved

Garlic Powder

Italian Seasonings

DIRECTIONS:

1. Preheat oven to 350°F and line a baking sheet with tinfoil.

2. Cut the baguette in half lengthwise then cut each length in half again. You should end up with four separate pieces.

3. Spread the tomato paste over each piece and sprinkle the desired amounts of garlic and seasonings over the top.

4. Lay the cherry tomatoes on top of each piece like a topping and sprinkle with cheese.

5. At this point you can freeze them if desired. They will keep about three weeks in a bag in the freezer.

6. Place in oven and cook for 10 - 15 minutes or until the cheese is melted and slightly browned.

7. Allow to cool completely before packing in a lunch box with a freezer pack to keep the pizza cool.

FRESH HAM SPRING ROLLS WITH SWEET DIPPING SAUCE

Spring rolls are a quick, easy and healthy lunch that everyone can enjoy. This recipe offers a fresh taste that is easily adjustable to the tastes of each child.

Serves 4 people

INGREDIENTS:

ROLL

½ cup thinly sliced ham (omit for vegetarian option)

1 carrot, peeled and grated

1 red bell pepper

6 red or green cabbage leaves

12 small rice paper wrappers

DIPPING SAUCE

2 tbsp tomato sauce (fresh or canned)

1 tbsp teriyaki sauce

1 tsp soy sauce

1 tsp honey

DIRECTIONS:

1. Wash vegetables to remove any pesticides and contaminants then dry thoroughly.

2. Take the lettuce and thinly shred it into a bowl; place the grated carrot into another bowl.

3. Next, cut the pepper into fourths and discard the membrane and the seeds. Slice it into thin pieces and set aside.

4. Lastly, slice the ham into ¼ inch long strips and also set aside.

5. Fill a large glass bowl with warm water and take out a cutting board.

6. Carefully dip a rice paper wrapper into the water, removing when soft and allowing excess water to drain off before setting onto the prepared drying area.

7. Keep in mind that the wrapper will continue to get softer the longer it is wet so try not to tear it by accident.

8. Now it is finally time to start making the rolls.

9. With your damp rice paper wrapper on the cutting board, carefully lay your ingredients in the center of the circle leaving at least two inches around the edge.

10. From there, pull the end closest towards you and wrap it over the ingredients, tucking it under them.

11. Then pull the next two closest sides over on top of that and slowly roll the wrap away from you.

12. Place on a plate seam side down and repeat steps 6 to 12 with remaining ingredients.

13. Serve immediately or, if sending in a lunch, refrigerate until use.

14. For easy transport, pack the sauce in sealed container and wrap rolls in plastic wrap; pack with an ice pack to prevent spoilage.

GINGER CHICKEN SPRING ROLLS

This fresh take on spring rolls offers a bit of sweetness and spice from the peppers and ginger and balances that out with the light, crisp taste of cucumbers, bean sprouts and lettuce. It is a light, yet filling meal that is sure to please.

Makes 4 servings

INGREDIENTS

12 large, round rice paper wrappers

1 head of lettuce, leaves separated, washed and removed

24 oz shredded or thinly sliced chicken

1 red bell pepper, de-seeded and thinly sliced.

1 cucumber, thinly grated

½ cup bean sprouts

1 knob of ginger, peeled and finely minced

1 clove of garlic, peeled and finely minced

DIRECTIONS:

1. Lightly oil a pan and put on medium high heat.

2. Add in peppers, garlic and ginger and cook until soft.

3. Add the chicken and toss until warmed then place in a bowl and set aside. At this point your house should smell delicious.

4. Fill a shallow dish half full with warm water and carefully dip a rice paper wrapper into the water.

5. Remove and allow some of the water to run off before laying down on a clean surface.

6. Remember that the longer it is wet the softer it will be so be careful not to tear.

7. Lay a lettuce leaf in the center of the wrap, leaving at least 2" on each side.

8. Place the chicken and pepper mixture, the cucumber and the bean sprouts in the center of the leaf.

9. Take the side closest to you and pull it over the filling and tuck under then fold in the next closest edges before rolling and laying it seam down on a plate.

10. Cover with a moist dish towel and repeat steps 4 - 9 with the remaining ingredients.

11. Cut in halves and refrigerate.

12. Send to school with your favorite dipping sauce in an insulated lunch box or one with a freezer pack to keep cool.

13. If the school allows it, ask for your rolls to be stored in a school refrigerator before eating.

GOOEY BACON BISCUIT

An excellent side dish to soup on a cold day, these biscuits are easy to make and easy to pack in your children's lunch box.

Makes 24

INGREDIENTS:

2 cups self-rising flour

1 tsp sugar

¼ tsp salt

2 tbsp butter

4 slices bacon, diced and cooked

1 cup cheese, grated

¾ cup milk or kefir.

DIRECTIONS:

1. Preheat oven to 400°F.

2. Line a baking sheet with tinfoil and grease with either butter or non-stick cooking spray

3. Sift the flour into a large mixing bowl before adding the salt and sugar. Stir to combine.

4. Using your fingertips, rub the butter into the flour. It will be crumbly and your hands will get very oily doing this.

5. When it crumbly and no noticeable chunks of butter or patches of flour remain add in the bacon and cheese.

6. Once added, cut the milk into the dough until you are able to stir it properly.

7. This dough will be sticky but heavy and hard to stir.

8. Once combined, turn out on a floured surface and knead slightly.

9. Pat the dough out gently to about 1" thickness. Do not roll or pat too hard or your biscuits will come out too dense.

10. Cut out with a floured round cookie cutter and place each cut out on the prepared cookie sheet.

11. Brush with milk and bake for 20 - 25 minutes or until golden brown.

12. Store in an airtight container.

13. When preparing your child's lunch, pack these biscuits carefully to avoid them being crushed.

14. If you are sending soup to school ensure that it is heated well before placing in a wide mouthed plastic vacuum flask.

15. Remember to add a cup and spoon for serving.

GREEN CHEESY MUFFINS

Either as a side item or the main meal, this muffin is a delicious addition to any lunchbox. A little butter or even some red sauce makes this a unique lunch item any child will love.

Makes 9 servings

INGREDIENTS:

9 oz butter, melted

¾ milk or kefir

2 cups self-rising flour

2 eggs

2 tbsp pesto sauce

¼ cup parmesan cheese, grated

Salt and pepper to taste

DIRECTIONS:

1. Preheat oven to 350°F. Spray a muffing tray with non-stick spray and set aside

2. In a medium sized bowl or a mixer, combine the flour, pesto, cheese and seasonings.

3. Make a slight indentation in the center of the dry ingredients and add in the wet ingredients.

4. Either gently mix with mixer or fold together with a spoon.

5. Do not over mix or the muffins will be too heavy.

6. Pour the finished batter into the prepared muffin tray and cook for 15 - 20 minutes

7. Serve warm or cool completely and pack a couple into the lunch box the next day.

GREEN TORTILLA WRAP

Wraps are easy to make and easy to pack and these wraps combine healthy proteins, healthy fats and the nutrients of green vegetables.

Makes 4 wraps

INGREDIENTS

1½ cups cooked chicken, shredded

$1/_3$ cup mayonnaise

2 shallots, finely sliced

1 avocado, flesh diced.

2 green onions, chopped

4 corn or flour tortillas

2 oz baby spinach

1 cup cheese of preference

Seasonings (optional)

DIRECTIONS:

1. In a large bowl, combine the chicken, mayonnaise, shallots, green onion and avocado.

2. Add in any seasonings you want. Salt and pepper are good staples but some turmeric, chili powder, paprika or garlic powder would also impart interesting flavors to the dish.

3. In each tortilla lay about a quarter of the cheese in the middle and then top with the avocado mixture and then the spinach.

4. Tightly roll and lay seam side down on a greased grill or a griddle.

5. Cook for 2-3 minutes or until lightly toasted. Then flip and repeat on the other side of the wrap.

6. Repeat steps 2 and 3 for the remaining ingredients.

7. If not serving these wraps immediately, cool completely and place in the fridge in a covered container.

8. Refrigerate overnight.

9. The next morning pack one carefully in a rigid container and send to school in an insulated lunch box.

10. If possible store in the school fridge until lunch time.

GRILLED OPEN-FACED TUNA SALAD SANDWICH

While tuna salad is good, sometimes your kids just want something different. Adding grilled cheese to the tuna, this is the perfect change to your usual lunchtime meal.

Makes 10 muffins

INGREDIENTS:

1 packet English muffins

1-7oz can of tuna, drained

3 tbsp mayonnaise

¼ cups grated carrot

¼ cup corn kernels

¼ cup celery, finely chopped

½ cup cheese, grated

Salt and pepper

Paprika

DIRECTIONS:

1. Add everything except the English muffins to a bowl and stir to mix.

2. This will be very lumpy so don't try to get it smooth. Just make sure everything is incorporated.

3. Heat up a skillet or frying pan and melt a tablespoon of butter in the center.

4. Cut the muffins in half and spoon some of the mixture onto each half.

5. Sprinkle with more cheese and place on the hot skillet.

6. Cook until the cheese is melted and the muffin is slightly browned.

7. Serve whilst still hot, or cool and refrigerate overnight.

8. Pack carefully into an insulated lunch box the next morning with the cheesy side up.

9. These are yummy cold and do not need to be reheated before eating.

HOMEMADE HEALTHY SPAGHETTI-O RECIPE

Most kids love spaghetti-o's. But those canned options often have disturbing ingredients and not enough health benefits to justify the purchase. This recipe is both tasty and healthy, giving your kids what they want and allowing you to feel good about what you're feeding them.

Serves 6

INGREDIENTS:

1 box pasta rings

1-16 oz can tomato sauce

1-8 oz can tomato paste

1 cup fresh or frozen spinach

1 red bell pepper, seeds removed and roughly chopped

1 carrot, chopped

1-2 tbsp water

2 oz shredded cheese (cheddar preferred)

Seasonings (garlic powder, salt, pepper, etc.)

DIRECTIONS:

1. Cook the pasta rings according to box directions. Drain and set aside.

2. In a small sauce pan, pour in the tomato sauce, tomato paste and any seasonings desired.

3. Cook over medium heat until bubbling, stirring occasionally to prevent burning.

4. Once bubbling, add cheese until melted then lower heat to simmering.

5. Using a blender or food processor, blend the spinach, pepper, carrot and water until it forms a paste.

6. If it is very liquid that is fine so long as there are no big chunks of vegetables.

7. If it is not blended enough, try adding more water.

8. Add in blended vegetables to tomato mixture and stir to incorporate.

9. Take off of heat. Add in pasta and gently mix until everything is mixed.

10. Serve immediately or leave to cool.

11. The next morning warm the spaghetti in the microwave or a saucepan and spoon into a wide mouthed vacuum flask. Seal well.

12. This dish does not contain meat or eggs and can be eaten directly from the vacuum flask. Just remember to pack a plastic spoon!

INDIAN FLATBREAD

Wraps are easy and popular for lunch but you can't always trust the preservatives in the store bought kind. This Indian bread is much like a tortilla but is very easy to make and very healthy.

Makes 4 servings

INGREDIENTS:

1 cup whole wheat flour

Pinch of salt

1 tbsp olive oil

3 tbsp water

DIRECTIONS:

1. In a medium sized bowl, toss the flour and salt together well. Sift if necessary.

2. Form a well in the center and pour in the olive oil and water, stirring carefully until all the flour is incorporated and it begins to form dough.

3. Knead this dough until smooth. When the dough is smooth and you can press into it with it springing back immediately you are ready for the next step

4. Roll the dough into four balls and use a rolling pin to roll them out flat. A tortilla press also works well for this.

5. Heat a frying pan over medium heat and place the dough into the pan.

6. These are very thin so it should only take about a minute on each side for it to be done.

7. These can be used like tortillas. Simple roll vegetables or meats up into them and send them along in an insulated lunch box.

LEBANESE CHEESY TOAST

Perfectly complimented by hummus or tahini, this is a lovely substitute for grilled cheese that your kids will adore.

Serves 4

INGREDIENTS:

4 slices Lebanese bread

1 tbsp butter

1 cup parmesan cheese, grated

DIRECTIONS:

1. Preheat oven to 350°F.

2. Spread the butter over each piece of butter then sprinkle liberally with the parmesan cheese.

3. Make sure each piece of bread has equal amounts of cheese.

4. Cut each piece of bread in half.

5. Cook on a baking sheet for 10 minutes or until cheese is melted and slightly browned.

6. Serve immediately or cool and store for up to three days.

7. Send to school in an insulated lunch box accompanied by a small container of hummus.

8. The toast can be dipped into the hummus as it is eaten.

OMELET QUICHE

Everyone likes an uncomplicated and flavorful recipe. This quiche combines simplicity with delicious ingredients to create a meal that your family will ask you for all the time.

Makes 3-4 servings

INGREDIENTS:

¾ cup white whole wheat flour

2 oz butter, melted

4 eggs, lightly beaten

2 cups of milk

1 onion, sliced

½ cup grated cheese

6 pieces of bacon, diced

2 mushrooms, sliced

1 zucchini, grated

¾ cup spinach

½ tsp dried basil or 8 basil leave finely chopped

DIRECTIONS:

1. Preheat oven to 350°F.

2. Grease a glass casserole dish with butter or non-stick spray and set aside.

3. In a bowl, blend the flour, eggs, and milk together using a slow mixing speed or a whisk.

4. Pour into the dish.

5. Toss the remaining ingredients in a separate bowl until combined.

6. Add to the flour mixture, mixing until evenly distributed.

7. Spoon into the dish and place it in the oven.

8. Bake for one hour.

9. This quiche should form a lovely crush out of the filling and the smell will bring your whole family to the kitchen.

10. Do not be surprised if all of it disappears quickly and your kids are begging you for more.

11. If it lasts the initial demand, refrigerate overnight.

12. Pack carefully the next morning into a rigid container and place this in a lunch box next to a frozen juice bottle to keep it cool.

13. If likes the quiche may be warmed but you will have to ask your child's teacher to do this. A microwave will be fine!

ONION AND GARLIC SPINACH SPIRALS

This roll-up is an easy and delicious way of getting your kids to eat some greens with their lunch.

Makes 12 servings

INGREDIENTS:

DOUGH

1 cup warm water

1 packet yeast

1 tsp honey

2 cups whole wheat flour

1 cup all-purpose flour

1 tbsp olive oil

1 tsp. salt

FILLING

1 onion, diced

1 clove garlic, crushed

5 oz bacon, diced

1-8 oz frozen spinach, defrosted

4 oz feta

1 cup cheese

DIRECTIONS:

1. Preheat oven to 450°F.

2. In a small bowl, whisk together the water, yeast and honey then set aside to allow the yeast to activate.

47

3. It will begin to bubble and froth.

4. In a stand mixer equipped with a dough hook add in the flours, salt, oil and yeast mixture and allow the mixer to knead the dough for approximately 10 minutes.

5. The dough is done when it is soft and stretchy.

6. You should be able to press into it and have the indentation spring back immediately. If it doesn't knead it a little bit longer.

7. If the dough is too dry add a tablespoon of water at a time until the problem is corrected.

8. Place dough in an oiled bowl and allow to rise for 1 hour

9. In a frying pan, heat a little bit of oil and fry the onion and garlic until soft then add the bacon and continue to cook.

10. Lastly, add in the spinach and mix until everything is heated through and warm.

11. Season as desired and spoon into a bowl. Mix in feta cheese.

12. Roll the risen dough into a large rectangle.

13. Spread the spinach mixture over the dough then sprinkle with half of the cheese.

14. Roll up long ways and lay seam down on a greased baking sheet.

15. Cut into 12 even pieces, place each piece on a prepared baking sheet and sprinkle with the remaining cheese.

16. Cook until golden, for 12 - 15 minutes

17. Freeze for lunch boxes.

18. The frozen spirals may be placed directly into the lunch box and will have time to defrost by lunchtime.

19. Put a freezer pack in if it is a very hot day.

OPEN-FACED GRILLED CHEESE

Perfect for an easy meal to prepare ahead of time, this stores easily and is good for making on a rushed morning.

Makes 6 servings

INGREDIENTS:

6 thick slices of white or wheat bread, frozen

7 oz butter, softened

4 oz grated parmesan cheese

Cooking spray

DIRECTIONS:

1. In a mixer, combine the butter and cheese until they are smooth and creamy.

2. Spread this over each piece of the bread then put the bread into the freezer.

3. Spray a frying pan or griddle with cooking spray and heat over medium high.

4. Put the cold toast on it butter side down until the top is completely thawed and the cheese is lightly browned.

5. Allow to cool.

6. Send to school in an insulated lunch box or one with a freezer pack to keep cool.

7. There should be no need to refrigerate these open sandwiches.

ORANGE PHYLLO ROLLS

The use of phyllo pastry makes this a light weight, delicious meal while the inclusion of the orange vegetables makes it a vitamin A powerhouse that your children will love.

Makes 10 rolls

INGREDIENTS:

1 sweet potato, peeled and cubed

1 pie pumpkin, flesh cubed

1 carrot, cubed

1 red bell pepper, seeds removed and cubed

3 green onions, sliced

2 oz feta cheese, crumbled

3 oz ricotta cheese, crumbled

4 oz cheddar cheese, shredded

1 tbsp basil, finely chopped

1 egg, lightly beaten

10 phyllo pastry sheets

DIRECTIONS:

1. Line a baking tray with tinfoil and grease with non-stick cooking spray or oil.

2. Place the vegetables in one layer on the tray and cook at 400ºF for approximate 20 minutes or until golden brown and soft.

3. Leave to cool.

4. If you would like, you can season the vegetables with herbs for a different taste.

5. Nutmeg and cinnamon can impart an interesting flavor as can garlic and sage.

6. In a bowl, combine vegetables, green onions, cheeses, basil and egg. Mix together as evenly as possible.

7. Carefully cut the phyllo sheets in half crossways.

8. Be very careful. Phyllo pastry is extremely fragile and will break easily.

9. Lightly spray each sheet with an oil spray and then fold in half.

10. Place approximately 1 tablespoon of mixture about an inch from the top of the dough.

11. Fold in the sides and roll up so that the filling is completely encased in the pastry.

12. On another lined, greased baking tray, place the roll seam down and bake at 400ºF for approximately 15 minutes or until slightly brown.

13. Be careful not to burn.

14. Serve immediately if they won't wait, otherwise refrigerate.

15. Send to school with a dipping sauce in an insulated lunch box or one with a freezer pack to keep cool.

16. The pastry sheets won't be as crispy as when first cooked but they will still taste amazing!

PIZZA POPPERS

Pizza is a popular item for kids but it is not always easily packed. These poppers are mini pizzas that can easily serve as a meal at home or on the go.

Makes 48 poppers

INGREDIENTS:

1 packet wonton wrappers

2 cups pizza or marinara sauce

1 cup shredded mozzarella

½ a green pepper, seeds removed and chopped finely

Seasonings (garlic powder, Italian seasonings, salt etc.)

Sausage, crumbled or finely chopped (optional)

Pepperoni, diced finely (optional)

Water (for sealing wrappers)

DIRECTIONS:

1. In a small sauce pan combine sauce, peppers and seasonings and meats (if desired).

2. Heat to bubbling then reduce heat to medium and add in the mozzarella.

3. Once the cheese is thoroughly melted remove from burner.

4. Lay out a wonton wrapper on a cutting board and carefully spoon a tablespoon of filling into the center.

5. Dip your finger in water and run it along the edge of the wrapper.

6. Fold over and press the edges to seal. Repeat this for remaining wrappers.

7. At this point the poppers can be frozen on a tray.

8. Once frozen, they can be stored in a bag in the freezer for up to one month.

9. If cooking immediately, heat the oven to 375°F and spray a cooking sheet with non-stick spray.

10. Lay out the desired amount of poppers and cook for 12-15 minutes or they are golden and crispy.

11. Leave to cool for 5 - 10 minutes before serving as the filling will be extremely hot.

12. Refrigerate the leftovers.

13. When packing into the lunch box separate each one with a piece of wax wrap.

14. Place the lunch box in an insulated container.

15. If the poppers contain meat, please ask for them to be kept in the school fridge until time to eat.

16. They can be warmed in a microwave if it is a chilly day but you will have to ask your teacher to do this.

17. Be careful as the filling will be hot!

PIZZA ROLL-UPS

These roll-ups are a perfect finger food for smaller children who have trouble with pizza slices and for packing in older children's lunch boxes.

Make 3 servings

INGREDIENTS:

1 cup whole wheat flour

1 cup all-purpose flour

3 tsp baking power

1 tsp salt

3 oz butter

$2/_3$ cup milk or kefir

Flour for dusting

3 tbsp tomato paste

1 cup grated cheese

1 egg lightly beaten

5 oz toppings (ham, bacon, green pepper, pepperoni etc.) (Optional)

Seasonings (optional)

DIRECTIONS:

1. Preheat oven to 400°F.

2. Line a baking tray with parchment paper or tin foil and grease.

3. In a large bowl, sift the flour, salt and baking powder.

4. Then, using your fingertips, rub the butter into the flour until it is crumbly.

5. Add in the milk, cutting it in with a knife or pastry blender until full incorporated.

6. You are finished when the mixture begins to hold together on its own.

7. At this point, turn the dough onto a floured counter top and knead for about five minutes until smooth.

8. If you have a mixer with a dough hook you can also knead that way.

9. If the dough remains sticky, add a bit more flour and knead to incorporate.

10. Roll the dough out into a rectangle.

11. Spread the tomato paste over it and season if desired.

12. Sprinkle with cheese and whatever toppings you may like.

13. Roll up length wise and slice into 10 - 12 pieces.

14. Lay these pieces on the tray and brush with the beaten egg.

15. Cook for 25 minutes.

16. Eat whilst warm and if by any chance there are any left over, refrigerate overnight.

17. The next morning, pack a couple of slices into a lunch box with a small fresh salad and send off to school in an insulated container to keep everything cool until lunch time.

18. If the toppings contain meat, please ask for them to be kept in the school fridge until time to eat.

PUFFY SWEET TUNA QUICHE

One of these little quiches makes an excellent midday snack, while three or four of them make a perfect lunch or dinner idea.

Makes 8 servings

INGREDIENTS:

1 large sweet potato, peeled and cubed

1 cup creamed corn

½ cup tuna

½ cup grated cheddar cheese

1 egg

2 sheets frozen puff pastry, thawed

DIRECTIONS:

1. Preheat oven to 350°F and spray a muffin pan with non-stick spray.

2. In a small bowl, cook the potato in the microwave for about 3-4 minutes or steam it for about 15 minutes, until soft.

3. Mash the potato and stir in the corn, tuna cheese and egg. Mix well and set aside.

4. Take the thawed pastry and cut it into 8 circles.

5. Press each circle into the muffin tin holes making sure not to break them.

6. Fill the pockets with the tuna and sweet potato mixture and bake for about twenty minutes or until golden brown.

7. If you like, you can sprinkle with cheddar cheese after 15 minutes of baking.

8. Cool and refrigerate overnight if making ahead.

9. Place the number of mini quiches required in a rigid lunch box.

10. Place in an insulated container or with a cool brick.

11. Please ask for them to be kept in the school fridge until time to eat.

12. Enjoy for lunch with some mini tomatoes.

13. There is no need to reheat this as the taste is just as good hot or cold.

SANDWICH ROLL UPS

Sandwiches are easy to make and send but they can also get boring day after day. This recipe is a new twist on a lunch time favorite.

Makes 2 servings

INGREDIENTS:

2 slices whole wheat bread

4 slices ham, very thinly sliced

Cream cheese

DIRECTIONS:

1. Remove the crusts from the bread and roll flat with a rolling pin or your hands.

2. The bread should be thin but be careful not to tear.

3. Spread desired amount of cream cheese on top of it then layer two pieces of ham on each piece of bread.

4. Take each piece of bread and roll one end to the other.

5. Cut into three pieces and press back together to form a log. This can then be wrapped up in either tinfoil or wax paper to help keep them together for travel.

6. Store with an ice pack in a lunch box to prevent cream cheese spoilage, particularly during warm weather.

7. This sandwich roll up can also be made with turkey or chicken slices instead of ham.

SAUCY BACON ROLL UPS

A perfect accompaniment to soup on a cold winter's day or a lovely summer time lunch, this recipe is perfect for your little ones lunch.

Preparation time: 10 minutes

Cook time: 12 minutes

INGREDIENTS:

2 packets of crescent roll dough

12 pieces of bacon, cooked

3 cups shredded mozzarella (or other preferred cheese)

Butter, melted (optional)

Garlic powder (optional)

Pizza or Marinara Sauce, for dipping

DIRECTIONS:

1. Preheat oven to 350°F.

2. Line a baking sheet with parchment paper or tin foil and grease with non-stick spray.

3. Open cans of crescent roll dough and carefully remove but do not break apart.

4. Lay out on a flat surface and, using a rolling pin; carefully make it into one big sheet of dough, keeping it in the rectangle shape.

5. Repeat with the other can.

6. Lay the bacon all along the dough evenly then sprinkle generously with cheese.

7. Roll from one end to the other to trap all the ingredients inside.

8. At this point, you can brush tops with melted butter and lightly sprinkle with garlic.

9. This will add some taste and make your house smell amazing.

10. Cut in 1" segments from end to end and place each piece on the greased baking sheet.

11. You can sprinkle more cheese on top if you would like.

12. Put in oven and bake for 11 - 12 minutes or until golden brown.

13. Serve immediately with pizza or marinara sauce or cool and refrigerate overnight for school.

14. Place the roll ups carefully in a container and pack together with a frozen juice bottle.

15. This should stay cold until lunch time.

16. If the weather is very warm you could place both the food and drink inside an insulated container.

SAVORY PUMPKIN MUFFINS

Pumpkin is a popular fall food but it is usually combined with sugar. This recipe offers a new way to experience a fall favorite without all the added sugars.

Makes 12 servings

INGREDIENTS:

1-10 oz can of pumpkin

2 cups self-rising flour

¼ cup preferred oil

2 eggs

1 cup cheese, grated

DIRECTIONS:

1. Preheat oven to 350°F and grease a muffin pan with non-stick spray. Set aside.

2. In a large bowl or mixer, combine the pumpkin, oil and eggs.

3. Mix until combined.

4. Slowly add in flour, stirring constantly, then add the cheese and continue to mix until just combined.

5. You should be able to see cheese strewn throughout the batter but not chopped up.

6. Pour batter into muffin tins and sprinkle with extra cheese if desired.

7. Bake for 20 - 25 minutes or until an inserted knife comes out clean.

8. Cool and place in an airtight container if not eaten immediately.

9. Send to school in a rigid lunch box to prevent the muffins being squashed!

SIESTA MUFFINS

A lovely twist on a southern favorite! Siesta Muffins combine the tastiest aspects of southwestern cuisine into an easily transportable form.

Makes 12 muffins

INGREDIENTS:

1 package cornbread mix plus ingredients to prepare it

6 slices of bacon, cooked and diced

1 cup creamed corn

1 cup grated cheese

¼ cup green onions, finely chopped

DIRECTIONS:

1. Preheat oven to 400°F.

2. Grease a muffin pan and set aside.

3. Prepare the cornbread mix according to directions. Mix in the cheese, bacon, corn, and onions and stir to fully combine.

4. Pour into the muffin tins evenly, shaking a bit to make the tops even.

5. Put the pan into the oven and cook for 15 - 20 minutes or until an inserted knife comes out clean.

6. Cool if not serving at once.

7. Place in a fridge until you are ready to put together the school lunches.

8. Pack the muffins in an insulated lunch box and send the youngsters off to school with some cherry tomatoes and carrot sticks to enjoy with their muffins.

SMALL CHICKEN AND VEGETABLE PIZZA

Pizza is always a favorite lunch item. But why purchase expensive pre-made pizzas when you can make one to your taste? This recipe is healthy and easily customizable to you and your family's preferences.

Makes two pizzas

INGREDIENTS:

2 pizza crusts (whole wheat preferably)

1 cup barbecue sauce or barbecue pizza sauce

16 cups cooked chicken, chopped.

1 green bell pepper, cored and thinly sliced

1 cup mushrooms, sliced

½ onion, peeled and sliced

1 cup cheddar cheese, grated

1 cup mozzarella cheese, grated

DIRECTIONS:

1. Preheat oven to 400°F and spray 2 pizza trays or large baking tray with non-stick spray and lay pizza crusts on pans.

2. Spread ½ the barbecue sauce evenly over each crust.

3. Scatter half the chicken on each pizza then lay the pepper, onions and mushrooms on top.

4. In a small bowl, mix the different cheeses together then sprinkle half the mixture over each pizza.

5. At this point the pizza can be frozen.

6. If cooking immediately, bake for 20 minutes or until the cheese is slightly browned.

7. Slice into sixths and serve immediately or cool and refrigerate overnight.

8. Place either the cooled or frozen pizza slices in an insulated lunch box for transporting to school.

9. If frozen the slices should defrost by lunchtime.

10. If just cooled it would be good to place a freezer brick alongside them to keep them fresh and cool.

SOUTHWESTERN CHILI SANDWICH

This sandwich offers a hefty dose of fiber and protein that will leave your loved ones feeling full and energized longer.

Makes 10 servings

INGREDIENTS:

20 oz cooked chicken, broken into pieces

¼ cup chili sauce, sweet or spicy

1-8 oz can kidney beans, drained and mashed

5 tomatoes, sliced

Cheddar cheese, shredded

20 slices high fiber white or whole wheat bread

DIRECTIONS:

1. Lay out two slices of bread on your counter top.

2. On one slice, spread the chili sauce evenly over the top.

3. On the other, spread the mashed beans.

4. Choosing one of the pieces, lay out the tomato and cooked chicken evenly, sprinkling with cheese.

5. Place the other piece of bread on top.

6. Repeat with remaining ingredients.

7. Can be served cold or slightly toasted.

8. These are best made on the morning they are to be eaten or otherwise the bread will go soggy especially if not toasted.

9. Cut the sandwiches in halves or quarters and carefully place them in an insulated lunch box.

10. These can be quite messy to eat and should be accompanied by a napkin to clean sticky fingers!

SPICY CHEESE ROLLS

Delicious with a hint of spice, these little bites are perfect for kids of all ages. Your children will be clamoring for more.

Makes 12 servings

INGREDIENTS:

1 package puff pastry

6 oz cream cheese, softened

4 oz cheddar cheese

¼ cup green chilies chopped

½ onion, finely chopped

¼ teaspoon sweet or spicy chili sauce

DIRECTIONS:

1. Preheat oven to 400°F. Line a baking sheet with tinfoil and grease with non-stick spray.

2. In a small bowl, beat the cream cheese until is a little bit fluffy.

3. At this point mix in the cheddar cheese, chilies, onions and sauce. Mix with a spoon until everything is equally combined and coated.

4. Lay out one of the puff pastry sheet on the counter or a cutting board.

5. Spread the cream cheese mixture over the pastry, leaving an inch on one end clear.

6. Roll up from the opposite side and use a bit of water on the plain edge to seal.

7. Cut into pieces and lay on the prepared baking sheet. Repeat with remaining ingredients.

8. Bake for 12 - 15 minutes or until golden brown.

9. Remove from oven and serve or cool refrigerate overnight for school.

10. Send to school in an insulated lunch box or one with a freezer pack to keep the rolls cool.

11. These pastries will not be quite as crisp as when first baked but will taste wonderful and the children will enjoy them.

SPICY EGG WRAP

For children that like a bit of spice, this is a perfect lunch. It's filling, healthy, and easily customizable.

Makes 4 servings

INGREDIENTS:

3 hard boiled eggs, peeled

2 tbsp mayonnaise

½ teaspoon curry powder

Pinch of salt

4 wraps

1 cup lettuce, shredded

7 oz shredded ham

DIRECTIONS:

1. Mash eggs, curry and mayonnaise in a bowl with the pinch of salt.

2. Mix together until everything is evenly combined.

3. Spread curry mixture on each of the wraps and top with the lettuce and ham.

4. Fold in the top and bottom before carefully folding.

5. If packing, wrap in tinfoil to prevent the wrap from opening in the lunch box.

6. These wraps should be placed in a rigid lunch box alongside a freezer pack to keep them cool.

7. Especially important in hot weather because of the inclusion of ham and eggs.

8. Add a few vine tomatoes for color and flavor.

SQUASH PINWHEELS

A filling meal or delicious snack, these pinwheels will earn high praise from anyone who tries them.

Makes 24 servings

INGREDIENTS:

2-8 oz cans of pumpkin

2 tbsp olive oil

1 onion, diced

1 clove garlic, crushed

8 oz frozen spinach

8 oz feta cheese, crumbled

3 sheets frozen puff pastry, thawed

1 egg, beaten

DIRECTIONS:

1. Preheat oven 450°F.

2. Line a baking dish with tin foil and grease with non-stick cooking spray. Set aside.

3. Place oil in a frying pan and heat over medium high heat.

4. Add the onion and garlic, sautéing until aromatic and soft.

5. Add the spinach and continue to cook, stirring frequently to avoid burning.

6. When thoroughly heated and coated, put into a bowl.

7. Add in the pumpkin and stir until thoroughly combined.

8. Season with salt and pepper to taste.

9. Lay out the thawed pastry sheets on a dry, flat surface and cut in half.

10. You will then have six strips.

11. Place a sixth of the mixture on each of these strips, leaving a small space.

12. On one of the long edge, brush a bit of beaten egg.

13. Then, starting with the un-brushed side, roll and press down to seal.

14. Repeat this process with the remaining pastry.

15. Cut each roll into quarters and lay each piece seam side down on the greased baking sheet, and brush with egg.

16. Bake for 25 - 30 minutes or until puffy and slightly browned.

17. Serve hot immediately with preferred dipping sauce or cool and place in the fridge overnight for school.

18. Pack carefully into a ridged container to prevent the pastry from breaking.

19. Put the dipping sauce in a small container with a tightly fitting lid.

20. Place in a suitable insulated container to transport and keep the contents cool until lunch time.

SUCCULENT SUSHI

Sushi is a healthy and easy lunch food. The seaweed offers a variety of micro nutrients while the brown rice and avocado leave your little one feeling full for much longer.

Make 10-20 servings

INGREDIENTS:

10 cups short grain brown rice

15 cups water

1 ¼ cups of rice vinegar

10 toasted Nori sheets

3 carrots, peeled and grated

3 cucumbers, grated

1 avocado, flesh sliced

Extra water for brushing

DIRECTIONS:

1. In a large saucepan, place the water and rice and bring to a boil.

2. Turn down the heat and simmer covered for 15 - 20 minutes or until sticky. Be careful it does not burn.

3. Stir in the vinegar and pour into a bowl or onto a large plate and leave to cool before use.

4. On a cutting board, lay out one piece of toasted Nori.

5. Spread a thin layer of rice over the sheet, leaving a 1 - 2" space at the end of the roll.

6. On the end with rice, lay small amounts of the grated and sliced vegetables.

7. Brush the bare part of Nori with water to allow for a better seal.

8. Roll from the edge with the vegetable towards the bare Nori edge and then press at the end to allow the seal to form.

9. Once rolled, squeeze slightly to tighten then cut in half and store in cling wrap.

10. Lay seam down.

11. Serve immediately or refrigerate overnight for school.

12. Pack the sushi rolls carefully side by side in a rigid container and place in an insulated carrying box.

13. Remember the chop sticks and some soy sauce for a special treat!

SUMMER SQUASH CASSEROLE

Reminiscent of a baked omelet, this casserole is a delicious lunch addition that is easy to make and easy to pack.

Serves 4

INGREDIENTS:

3 zucchini, grated

3 yellow squash, grated

1 onion, grated

1 potato, grated

1 carrot, grated

8 slices of bacon, chopped

1 cup of shredded cheddar cheese

1½ cups flour

6 eggs, slightly beaten

Salt and pepper

DIRECTIONS:

1. Preheat oven to 350°F.

2. Using butter or non-stick spray, grease a casserole dish and set aside.

3. In a large bowl, mix all ingredients until well combined.

4. Pour into the prepared dish.

5. If you desire, you can sprinkle with extra cheese or even bread crumbs for an extra crunch.

6. Cook for 1 hour and 25 minutes.

7. Slice and serve warm or cool well and refrigerate overnight.

8. The next morning place a slice in a rigid container along with a small fresh salad.

9. Put in lunch box alongside a freezer brick to keep everything cool.

10. Remember to pack a plastic fork to make eating easier.

SUMMER SQUASH CROQUETTES

Hash-browns are a popular food with kids, as are tater tots. These croquettes are very similar to those popular dishes but with all the health benefits of squash. Fry in coconut oil for a healthy dose of omega-3.

Makes 6 large croquettes

INGREDIENTS:

2 cups yellow squash (or zucchini), grated

1 cup onion, finely chopped

1 egg, beaten

½ cup green onion, finely chopped

1 tsp salt

1 tsp black pepper

½ tsp garlic powder

½ cup whole wheat flour

Coconut Oil (for frying)

DIRECTIONS:

1. In a medium bowl, combined all the ingredients except for the flour.

2. Stir well. Mix in the flour and stir again.

3. Take small portions of the mixture and squeeze together, forming small patties.

4. If you wish to make something more like a tater tot; take tablespoon sized portions and carefully squeeze together to make smack cylinders.

5. Do this until the mixture is gone.

6. At this point you can put them on a greased and lined cookie sheet to freeze, storing them in a plastic bag after they are frozen.

7. They will last about a month in the freezer.

8. If you want to serve them immediately, heat a large skillet or frying pan over medium-high heat.

9. Place approximately 1 - 2 tablespoons of coconut oil into the hot skillet and allow it to melt.

10. Place one of the patties in the pan.

11. Cook until browned (approximately 2 - 3 minutes) then flip over and repeat.

12. Once fully cooked, set on a paper towel covered plate to drain.

13. Serve hot and at home! These will never make it as far as a lunchbox!

14. Otherwise refrigerate overnight for school.

15. Send to school in an insulated lunch box.

16. Can be served with ketchup or other dipping sauces if desired.

17. Remember to pack this separately so that it will not spill all over the croquettes.

SWEET ASIAN CHICKEN

A wonderful answer to unhealthy, pre-made chicken wings, these drumsticks are deliciously sweet and moist. Your whole family will beg you to make these for lunch or dinner.

Makes 12 pieces

INGREDIENTS:

½ cup soy sauce

$^1/_3$ cup honey

1 lemon, juiced

1 garlic clove, crushed

12 chicken drumsticks

DIRECTIONS:

1. Preheat oven to 350°F and lightly grease a glass casserole dish or line a baking pan with foil.

2. Lay the drumsticks close together in a single layer in the pan or dish.

3. In a bowl, combine the garlic and liquid ingredients, stirring well.

4. Pour this marinade over the chicken so that it coats as much of it as possible.

5. Cover with tinfoil to prevent drying out then cook for 45 minutes.

6. Baste every 15 minutes with the marinade and take off the tinfoil for the last 10 minutes if you would like crispier chicken.

7. The meat is done when juices run clear after piercing the thickest part of the drumsticks.

8. Cool well before placing in the refrigerator overnight.

9. Pack carefully the next day and put in a cool box.

10. Remember plenty of napkins for those sticky fingers!

SWEET BEAN AND BEEF BURRITO

Offering a dose of whole grains and a good percentage of your kids' daily intake of vitamin C and protein, these burritos are a healthy and quick option for lunch or dinner.

Makes 4 servings

INGREDIENTS:

4 oz flank steak, sliced

3 oz cooked pinto beans, mashed

4 whole wheat or corn tortillas

2 cups shredded lettuce

2 small tomatoes, sliced

1 red bell pepper, seeded and thinly sliced

1 carrot, peeled and grated

1 tbsp sweet chili sauce

Grated cheese to taste

Non-stick spray

DIRECTIONS:

1. Lightly grease a large frying pan and place on high heat on the stove.

2. Take one-third of the flank steak and cook until brown and well done.

3. Place in a bowl and repeat with the remaining beef.

4. Lower the heat to medium high and place the red bell pepper slices into the pan.

5. Cook until soft before putting in a bowl and setting aside.

6. Take the wraps and slowly fill with ingredients leaving 1 - 2" space on each side.

7. Pull the side closest to you over the ingredients and the tuck the next closest sides over.

8. Finally, roll and lay seam side down on a plate.

9. Burritos can be served now with additional chili sauce.

10. Refrigerate overnight - built as above, or disassembled.

11. It would be best to then send these to school assembled on the day and wrapped in foil.

12. Place them in an insulated lunch box and add an extra cold source such as a frozen juice bottle to keep the burritos fresh.

13. These can also be wrapped in foil or wax paper and stored in the freezer for up to two weeks.

TOMATO CHIA SNACKS

Kids love pizza but often pizza flavored snacks are extremely unhealthy. These snacks offer wonderful health benefits and taste amazing. They are great with any lunch as a side dish.

Makes 25-30 servings

INGREDIENTS:

1 cup tomato or vegetable juice

1 cup Chia seeds

2 tbsp sesame seeds

$^2/_3$ cup pumpkin seeds

$^2/_3$ cup sunflower seeds

¼ cup flax seeds

1¼ tsp sea salt

½ tsp garlic powder

½ tsp Italian spices

DIRECTIONS:

1. Preheat oven to 170°F and line a baking pan with parchment paper.

2. Mix chia seeds with the vegetable juice. It will form a lovely gel which is exactly what you want.

3. Add in the seasonings and stir until evenly distributed.

4. Mix in remaining ingredients. It may be hard to stir but make sure that everything is evenly combined.

5. With greased hand, scoop mixture from the bowl and put it in the prepared pan, spreading it as thinly as possible (¼ an inch thick is ideal).

6. Place in the oven for 60 - 70 minutes.

7. Then turn the mixture over and cook for another hour.

8. Turn off heat and leave the mixture in the oven over night to dry out.

9. In the morning, break the snacks into separate pieces and serve or store.

10. These tasty snacks can be placed in an ordinary lunch box as they are dry and biscuity!

TOWER OF GRILLED CHEESE

Balancing out the cheese with the tartness of tomato, this sandwich is a delicious and filling meal that is both easy and sure to please.

Makes 2 sandwiches

INGREDIENTS:

8 slices of bread (whole wheat preferred)

Butter

6 - 12 slices of cheddar or American cheese

6 - 12 tomato slices

DIRECTIONS:

1. Take four pieces of the bread and butter one side.

2. Place two pieces aside and the place the remaining two on a plate.

3. Stack 1 - 2 slices of cheese and 1 - 2 slices of tomato then top with a piece of none buttered bread.

4. Repeat twice more, topping the last cheese and tomato levels with the remaining butter bread.

5. Keep the buttered side up.

6. Heat up a griddle and melt a little bit of extra butter in it.

7. Add the sandwiches and cook on one side until the cheese is melted. Carefully flip over to the other side.

8. Do this until cheese is melted

9. Serve warm or let it cool down to pack for school.

10. You may want to cut this in half or press it down to fit it into an insulated lunch box.

11. Some crunchy celery sticks would go well with these sandwiches.

TRADITIONAL FALAFELS

A traditional Middle Eastern food, Falafel is a popular vegetarian staple. It has a healthy dose of protein and is easily paired with the same foods as meat dishes like tacos. This is a quick to make dish and is equally as easy to send in a lunch box for a healthy meal.

Makes 12

INGREDIENTS:

1-15 oz can chickpeas, drained and rinsed

1 medium onion, finely chopped

1 tbsp minced garlic

2 tbsp parsley

1 tsp coriander

¾ tsp cumin

½ tsp salt

2 tbsp flour

Oil for frying

DIRECTIONS:

1. In a food processor or blender combine all the ingredients except for the oil. Pulse to a thick paste.

2. Roll small balls from the paste and place on a covered pan before slightly flattening. Do this until all of the mixture is used.

3. In a large frying pan, heat the oil to a high temperature.

4. Fry the falafels until crispy but be sure not to burn as they will burn easily.

5. Serve on pita bread with tomatoes, lettuce, onion, sweet peppers and hummus dip.

6. Cool the falafels and refrigerate overnight if you are going to use them the next days for a luncheon surprise!

7. Make up the pitas just before packing the lunch boxes or keep the pita and falafels separate and serve with a side salad of the vegetables.

8. Send to school in an insulated lunch box to keep cool until munching time.

TUNA SALAD PITA WRAPS

Pita wraps are scrumptious and a portable lunch for anyone. This unique twist on tuna salad replaces mayonnaise with sour cream for a slightly tangy flavor.

Makes 12 servings

INGREDIENTS:

2-15 oz cans of tuna, drained

4 carrots, grated

2 stalks celery, finely chopped

½ head of lettuce, shredded

¼ cup Greek yogurt

12 slices pita bread

DIRECTIONS:

1. In a small bowl, combine the tuna, carrots, celery and sour cream until roughly mixed.

2. Lay out pita bread on a plate and spoon some of the mixture onto it, spreading slightly.

3. Sprinkle with lettuce and fold over.

4. Repeat with remaining ingredients.

5. Pack these in plastic wrap to hold all of the ingredients inside the pita.

6. Place in a rigid container and send to school with a frozen juice or cold brick next to it.

7. This will help to keep the tuna pita wraps fresh until ready to eat, or even better, see if you can also use the refrigerator at school until lunch.

VEGETABLE POCKETS

Hot pockets are often an easy lunch for kids but they are far from healthy. These fun to make pockets are just as easily transported and far healthier for your kids then anything pre-packaged.

Makes 12 servings

INGREDIENTS:

1 small sweet potato, peeled and coarsely chopped

1 small carrot, peeled and finely chopped

1 red potato, peeled and finely chopped

½ cup frozen peas

1 - 5 oz can corn, rinsed and drained

½ cup shredded cheddar

2 eggs, lightly beaten

3 sheets frozen short crust pastry, thawed

DIRECTIONS:

1. Preheat oven to 450°F.

2. Line a baking sheet with tinfoil or parchment paper and grease with non-stick spray or butter.

3. Using boiling water, cook the sweet potato until tender (about 10 minutes).

4. While you are doing this, place the carrot and potato in another pot and cook until tender (about 5 minutes).

5. Drain both pots and allow the vegetables to cool in a bowl until needed.

6. Once cool, combine potato mixtures.

7. Add in the peas, corn cheese and 1 of the eggs and stir to combine. Season as desired.

8. Using a large, round cookie cutter, cut 12 discs out of the pastry sheets and lay on the prepared baking sheet.

9. Spoon the vegetable mixture into each disk then brush the edges with beaten egg.

10. Fold in half and press the edges together to seal.

11. Brush with remaining egg and season with either sesame seeds or seasonings.

12. Cook for 15 minutes or until cooked through and golden.

13. Cool completely before refrigerating overnight.

14. These pastry parcels will squash in a packet so place them in a rigid container inside a cooler box for freshness and easy transportation.

VEGETABLE QUICHE

Good warm or cool, this quiche is a mouthwatering meal that travels well. Try a mixture of different vegetables to alter the taste and you'll find it to be highly versatile.

Serves 6

INGREDIENTS:

1 sheet frozen pie crust, thawed

2 tsp oil

1 medium onion, chopped

1 small red bell pepper, seeds removed and diced

1½ cups broccoli florets

1 cup cubed pumpkin or butternut squash

1 zucchini, sliced

1-5 oz can corn kernels, drained

3 eggs

¾ cup milk

1 tsp mustard

½ tsp salt

½ cup shredded cheese

DIRECTIONS:

1. Preheat oven to 350°F.

2. Grease a pie plate and place the pie crust in it, pressing down so that it is firmly against the glass.

3. Sprinkle with some of the cheese.

4. Heat a frying pan with the oil and cook the pepper and onion until they are soft.

5. Meanwhile, either in the microwave or in a pot, steam the broccoli, pumpkin and zucchini until soft.

6. Mix all the vegetable in a bowl with the corn.

7. In a separate bowl, whisk the eggs, milk, mustard and salt.

8. Spoon the vegetables into the pie plate and pour in the egg mixture.

9. Sprinkle with more cheese.

10. Cook for 30 minutes or until the eggs are completely set.

11. Cool and place in a refrigerator overnight and then slice into wedges.

12. Pack a wedge carefully into a rigid container and add a few slices of cucumber, chunks of tomato and the odd carrot stick to make a well rounded delicious lunch.

13. Pack in a container with a freezer brick to keep cool until eaten.

VEGGIE SILVER DOLLARS

Delicious when paired with yogurt or sour cream, this is a dish that's easily frozen and reheated during the hectic morning rush.

Makes 24

INGREDIENTS:

1 cup whole wheat flour

1 cup self-rising flour

6 eggs

4 - 5 cups grated zucchini and corn

½ - 1 cup grated cheese

Salt and pepper to taste

Milk

DIRECTIONS:

1. In a bowl, mix all the ingredients thoroughly.

2. Add in enough milk so that the mixture is the consistency of pancake batter

3. Add a tiny bit of olive oil to a frying pan and heat over medium high heat.

4. Drop a tablespoon of the batter into the pan and cook until both sides are browned.

5. Repeat with remaining batter.

6. Refrigerate overnight after letting these cool completely.

7. Send to school with a yogurt sauce mixed with a bit of chili powder or curry in an insulated lunch box.

8. They can be served cold for school and it would not be necessary to reheat them.

YUMMY CHICKEN SANDWICH

Here's a good balance of whole grain, proteins, and vegetables.

Makes 12 servings

INGREDIENTS:

2 lbs ground chicken

½ cup onion, chopped

½ cup celery, finely chopped

½ cup carrot, grated

Whole wheat hamburger bun

Lettuce

Tomatoes, sliced

Mayonnaise

Pickle slices

Seasonings (salt, pepper, paprika, garlic powder, etc.)

DIRECTIONS:

1. Put the meat into a bowl and season as desired.

2. Using your hands, blend the seasonings in then add the vegetables and continue to mix.

3. Form the meat into patties and place in the refrigerator for one hour to allow them to firm up.

4. This step keeps them from falling apart during the cooking process.

5. Grill or fry until cooked through the center. If there is pink it is not done.

6. Undercooked poultry can carry a host of bacteria so be sure to cook it thoroughly.

7. Place each burger on a bun and dress with lettuce, tomatoes, mayonnaise and pickles.

8. Refrigerate overnight.

9. If packing in a lunchbox, consider separating the salads from the chicken to prevent a soggy bun!

10. These will need to be kept cool until eaten, such as in the school refrigerator, especially on a hot day and it would be best to accompany them with a freezer brick next to their container.

ZUCCHINI BAKE

Another healthy use for summer time squash, this is a highly versatile recipe that is made all the more delicious by the inclusion of your favorite sausages.

Serves 4

INGREDIENTS:

3 zucchini, grated

1 red onion, chopped

1 carrot, grated

4 slices bacon, diced

2 cooked sausages, diced

1 cup cheese, grated

½ cup plain flour

3 eggs, lightly beaten

Salt and pepper

DIRECTIONS:

1. Preheat oven to 350°F.

2. Line a baking pan with tinfoil and spray with non-stick spray.

3. In a mixing bowl, combine all ingredients until everything is well mixed.

4. As this isn't a particularly thin mixture you will have to stir a great deal to make sure all vegetables and spices are evenly distributed.

5. Pour mixture into the prepared pan and bake for 55 - 60 minutes until eggs are set and the top is browned.

6. Cool completely and refrigerate overnight before cutting.

7. The zucchini bake contains meat and therefore it would be best to pack each piece in a piece of foil inside an insulated container.

8. This will keep the bake cool and fresh until the lunch bell rings!

9. To be super safe refrigerate them at school until eaten.

10. A plastic fork would help the munching process.

PART II: SWEET

APPLE CINNAMON BUNS

This recipe will bring your family running to the kitchen for seconds. Easy to make and easy to pack, this makes a perfect addition to any lunch.

Makes 8 servings

INGREDIENTS:

2¾ cups self-rising flour

1 tbsp dried yeast

2 tbsp caster sugar

2 oz butter, melted

½ cup milk, warmed

½ cup butter milk

1 medium red apple, cored and finely chopped

½ tsp ground cinnamon

¼ tsp ground nutmeg

¼ cup brown sugar

DIRECTIONS:

1. Preheat oven to 425°F.

2. Line a large baking pan with tinfoil and grease with butter or non-stick cooking spray then set aside.

3. In a mixer, combine the flour, yeast and sugar in a bowl. Stir gently to combine.

4. Add the butter, milk and butter milk carefully and mix on a low speed. Be very careful that your milk is not too hot.

5. Mix until a dough forms then lower to a kneading speed. A dough hook works well for this.

6. It is done when a small piece of it can be pulled apart without breaking and you can see light through it.

7. Leave to rise for 1 hour in a warm spot or until doubled in size.

8. Once risen; punch dough down and knead again for another 2 - 3 minutes. Then roll out into a large rectangle.

9. In a small bowl, combine the apple, cinnamon, nutmeg and sugar in a bowl.

10. Sprinkle this over the dough then roll up and lay seam down.

11. Cut into even slices and place in the tray.

12. Leave covered for 20 minutes to allow the dough to rise again.

13. Bake for 25 minutes or until the rolls are browned and cooked through.

14. The smell of cinnamon will have your family stealing bites so serve immediately.

15. Can be drizzled with maple syrup if desired.

16. If packing in a lunch box for school it would be better not to drizzle with the maple syrup!

17. Wrap in plastic wrap individually and pop into the lunch box as a special treat.

APPLESAUCE COOKIES

These cookies are a refreshing twist on a typical oatmeal cookie. Sweetened with apples, they're a sugary treat that is sure to please!

Makes 28 cookies

INGREDIENTS:

1 cup unsweetened applesauce

1 cup brown or coconut sugar

4 oz butter

1 cup whole wheat flour

½ cup all-purpose flour

1 egg

½ cup rolled oats

½ tsp salt

1 tsp baking soda

1 tsp cinnamon

½ tsp nutmeg

½ tsp cloves

½ cup coconut

DIRECTIONS:

1. Preheat oven to 375°F.

2. Line a baking tray with tin foil or parchment paper and grease with either butter or nonstick cooking spray.

3. In a mixer (or using a hand mixer) cream together the butter and sugar until light in color and sugar is not visually apparent.

4. Add in egg and continue to beat.

5. Once everything is combined, add in remaining ingredients and mix thoroughly with a wooden spoon, being careful not to beat the mixture.

6. The dough will be slightly thick and lumpy but this is okay as long as the flour is fully incorporated.

7. Place teaspoons of dough on the baking sheet with a space between them.

8. These cookies will spread and it could ruin the appearance if they blend together.

9. Place in the oven and cook for 13 - 15 minutes.

10. Leave to cool on a paper towel then serve.

11. These cookies can be stored in a plastic container for up to a week.

12. A couple of these cookies added to a savory lunch box will go down well.

AUTUMN APPLE CAKE

Apples are a healthy, popular food. This recipe combines the versatile fruit with a kid friendly dessert to create something the whole family will love.

Makes 6 servings

INGREDIENTS:

6 apples, peeled cored and diced

1 tbsp cinnamon

5 tbsp sugar

2¾ cup white whole wheat flour, sifted

3½ tsp baking powder

1 tsp salt

1 cup unsweetened apple sauce

1 cup brown or coconut sugar

¼ cup apple cider

2½ tsp vanilla extract

4 eggs

DIRECTIONS:

1. Preheat oven to 350°F and grease a cake or pie pan.

2. In a small bowl, toss the apples with cinnamon and sugar and put aside.

3. Next, put the dry ingredients in a mixing bowl and stir them until everything is evenly distributed.

4. In a separate bowl, do the same thing with the wet ingredients except the eggs.

5. Pour into the dry ingredients and stir.

6. Add in the eggs one by one, stirring continuously. A mixer on an appropriate speed would be helpful for this.

7. Once everything is properly combined, pour half of the mixture into the prepared pan then sprinkle with half of the apples.

8. Then pour the remaining batter on top and place the remaining apples on top of that.

9. If desired you can sprinkle with a little extra cinnamon and sugar.

10. Bake for an hour and a half or until an inserted knife comes out clean.

11. Leave to cool completely, and then serve.

12. This can be stored in the refrigerator for up to a week.

13. Cut into slices that are easy to handle if adding to a lunch box and wrap in plastic wrap to keep the cake fresh and everything else crumb free!

AUTUMN MUFFINS

Apple picking is a favorite fall activity. But what to do with all those extras! This recipe solves that problem and makes a perfect fall treat for the kids.

Makes 12 muffins

INGREDIENTS:

2 eggs

¼ cup brown or coconut sugar

½ cup unsweetened applesauce

1 cup apple, grated

2 tsp cinnamon

1 cup whole wheat flour

1 tsp salt

3 tsp baking powder

1 cup all-purpose flour

¾ tsp baking soda

DIRECTIONS:

1. Preheat oven to 400°F and then spray a muffin pan with non-stick spray.

2. You can use cupcake liners if you want to make smaller muffins however this is not necessary.

3. In a medium bowl or mixer, beat the eggs and sugar together for about one minute.

4. In a separate small bowl, stir together the baking soda and apple sauce. It may foam up but that is normal.

5. Add that mixture to the bowl and then add in the chopped apple and cinnamon.

6. In yet another bowl, mix the flours, baking powder and salt everything is incorporated.

7. Fold the flour mixture gently into the applesauce.

8. It is all right to use a slow mixing speed to do this if you're using a mixer but do not beat. If you beat the mixture, the muffins will turn out too dense.

9. Once the flour is just combined (it may look a little lumpy but this is normal) spoon into the muffin tin so that each space has an even amount.

10. If you like, sprinkle with a little extra cinnamon and sugar.

11. Bake for 20 minutes or until an inserted knife comes out clean.

12. Cool well before adding to your child's lunch for school. Wrap individually before sending off to school!

BANANA NUT MUFFINS

Sometimes the bananas you bought with good intentions don't get eaten before their time. But no need to throw them away! This recipe uses up those old, undesirable bananas to make a delicious treat the whole family will love.

Makes 12 muffins

INGREDIENTS:

1 egg

¼ cup caster sugar or fine coconut sugar

¼ cup unsweetened applesauce

7 oz yogurt

3 bananas, mashed

¼ cup walnuts

1 cup whole wheat flour

½ cup all-purpose flour

3 tsp baking powder

1 tsp salt

DIRECTIONS:

1. Preheat oven to 400°F and coat a muffin pan with non-stick spray.

2. In a medium bowl or mixer, beat together the egg, sugar oil and yogurt.

3. In another small bowl, mix the flours, salt and baking powder until well combined.

4. Gently fold in the bananas, walnuts and flour.

5. While you may use a mixer to stir (at a low setting) do not beat as this will make the muffins too dense.

6. Once the mixture is just combined (it will be lumpy) spoon into prepared tin in equal amounts.

7. Cook for 30 minutes or until an inserted knife comes out clean.

8. Remove from tins and leave to cool before serving.

9. These individual treats should be wrapped separately from anything savory in the lunch box to keep the flavors separate and allow for maximum enjoyment.

BASIC PIKELET RECIPE

This versatile alternative to pancakes is great to pack in school lunches or serve as breakfast. They can even make an interesting dinner item if combined with more savory sauces and side dishes.

Makes 20

INGREDIENTS:

2 cups whole wheat flour

1 tsp baking powder

½ tsp salt

$1/_3$ cup caster sugar

1 egg

1 cup milk or kefir

1 tbsp butter

DIRECTIONS:

1. In a large bowl or mixer, sift the flour, salt and baking powder then add sugar and drop in the egg.

2. Stir until well combined.

3. Slowly add in enough milk to make a smooth batter. It should still be thick even when fully combined.

4. Heat a skillet and melt in it ½ a teaspoon of coconut oil.

5. Drop tablespoons of batter into the pan.

6. Multiple amounts can be cooked at the same time; however if you are worried about burning them take it one at a time until you feel more comfortable.

7. Brown one side then flip to brown the other.

8. Remove from heat and cover with a paper towel.

9. Repeat with remaining batter and serve immediately.

10. Can be served with syrup, butter or fruit topping.

11. For the lunch boxes, sandwich 2 pikelets together with butter and just a little syrup or honey.

12. Wrap well as they may leak a little and send along a napkin for sticky fingers!

BATTER FRIED BANANAS

Fried food is popular among children but is often unhealthy. These little disks offer all the flavor of fried foods with far more health benefits.

Makes 12

INGREDIENTS:

2 over-ripe bananas cut into thick slices

¼ cup whole wheat flour for dusting

1 cup whole wheat flour

1½ tsp baking powder

½ tsp salt

1 tbsp sugar

1 egg

¾ cup milk or kefir

2 oz butter, melted

DIRECTIONS:

1. In a small bowl, dust the banana slices with ¼ a cup of flour until they are fully coated.

2. To make the batter, combine the remaining flour, salt and baking powder, sifting if necessary.

3. Add in the egg, milk and sugar.

4. Once everything is in the bowl, whisk until thoroughly mixed and batter like.

5. Heat a frying pan on medium high heat and melt the butter in it.

6. When the pan is hot and thoroughly greased, dip the banana disks in the batter and fry until golden, flipping once.

7. Serve hot. Syrup can be used as a dip.

8. Although these are usually eaten hot, children love them cold as well and they make a great addition to a lunch box.

9. Pack in a separate little container with a lid and if using syrup pack separately to use as a dip.

BERRY BANANA BREAD

This is new twist on a healthy favorite. Kids will love the sweetness and you will feel good about giving it to them as a treat.

Makes 10 slices

INGREDIENTS:

$^2/_3$ cup of butter

¾ cup brown sugar or coconut sugar

2 eggs, lightly beaten

2 over ripe (brown) bananas, mashed

1½ cup whole wheat flour

½ cup all-purpose flour

1½ tsp baking powder

½ tsp salt

½ cup milk

½ cup fresh or frozen berries (raspberries, blueberries, cranberries, strawberries etc.)

DIRECTIONS:

1. Preheat oven to 350°F.

2. Line a 9 x 5 loaf pan with parchment paper or in foil and grease with either butter or non-stick spray. Set aside.

3. Cream together the butter and sugar until smooth an incorporated.

4. This may be done by hand however a mixer (either hand or stand) makes this process faster.

5. Once creamed, add in each egg one at a time, mixing each until incorporated and smooth.

6. Add in the mashed banana.

7. In a separate bowl, mix the remaining dry ingredients until everything is evenly distributed.

8. Add the flour ½ a cup at a time to the wet ingredients until it has all been incorporated and the mixture is smooth.

9. At this point it should resemble thick pancake batter.

10. Fold in the berries being very careful not to break them apart.

11. After the batter is ready, spoon into the loaf pan and jiggle the pan until the top is smooth.

12. Put into the oven for 45 - 50 minutes or until an inserted knife comes out clean.

13. By this point the room should smell wonderful and any one in the house may be hovering around the kitchen.

14. Remove the bread from oven and leave to cool on a wire rack before slicing.

15. Eat immediately or freeze in individual sized portions.

16. Make sure that if freezing the bread is completely cool; slices should keep up to 2 months in the freezer.

17. Slices may be taken directly from the freezer and added to a lunch box.

18. By the time the bell rings for recess the bread will have defrosted and be beautifully 'fresh'!

BERRY OATMEAL YOGURT

Yogurt can be a healthy start to the day, a healthy dessert or a healthy snack. Lightly sweetened it gives the effect of being sugary without the negative effects of eating too much sugar. This recipe offers not only a dose of protein that will leave you feeling full but also of calcium, vitamin C and fiber.

Makes 1 serving

INGREDIENTS:

2 tbsp oats

1 tbsp ground flaxseed

$1/3$ cup Greek or soy yogurt

2 tbsp honey

2 tbsp dried fruit of choice

Handful fresh or frozen berries

Sunflower seeds to taste

DIRECTIONS:

1. Combine first six ingredients in a small bowl.

2. Sprinkle with sunflower seeds and serve cold.

3. For a school lunch use a cup with a lid to transport the yogurt. Remember a plastic teaspoon!

4. Send this to school in a cool box with a freezer brick inside to keep it fresh, and then preferably store it in the schools refrigerator until eaten.

BLACK BEAN BROWNIES

This delicious recipe offers a hefty dose of protein and complex carbs. And no one will even know they're eating beans! These brownies are gluten free, dairy free and vegan to boot.

Makes 9 - 12 brownies

INGREDIENTS:

1-15 oz can black beans, drained and rinsed

2 tbsp cocoa powder

½ cup quick oats

¼ tsp salt

½ cup maple syrup

¼ cup coconut oil or vegetable oil

2 tsp vanilla extract

½ tsp baking powder

½ cup semi-sweet chocolate chips

DIRECTIONS:

1. Preheat oven to 350°F.

2. Line a baking pan with tinfoil or parchment paper and grease with non-stick spray.

3. In a food processor, combine all of the ingredients except for the chocolate chips and blend.

4. Pour mixture into the baking pan.

5. If desired, you can sprinkle more chocolate chips on the top.

6. Cook for 10 - 15 minutes then leave to cool for ten minutes.

7. Cut and serve.

8. Wrap individually and place in a lunch box.

BREAKFAST CAKE

Cake is a childhood favorite but is often not particularly healthy. However this recipe adds in some healthy elements that can make a tasty snack for lunch or after dinner as well as a lovely accompaniment to breakfast.

Serves 24

INGREDIENTS:

8 oz butter

1 cup brown or coconut sugar

4 eggs

4 bananas, mashed

15 oz plain yogurt

2 cups whole wheat flour

$^2/_3$ cup all-purpose flour

3 tsp baking powder

DIRECTIONS:

1. Preheat oven to 350°F.

2. Line a 9 x 9 or round cake pan with foil and grease using butter or non-stick spray.

3. In a large bowl or mixer, cream together butter and sugar until smooth and creamy.

4. To this mixture add eggs one at a time, beating well between each addition.

5. Fold in bananas and yogurt, be careful not to over stir.

6. In another bowl, sift together the dry ingredients.

7. Once properly combined, fold into the wet mixture until just combined.

8. Pour into the prepared tin and bake for 40-50 minutes or until an inserted knife come out clean.

9. Be warned, the smell of cooking bananas will bring everyone to the kitchen!

10. Cut and serve or the cake will keep in the refrigerator for a week.

11. This popular cake may not even make it to the lunchboxes!

12. If it does, wrap each piece in plastic wrap before adding to the rest of the lunch treats.

CHOCOLATE KEFIR CHIA SEED PUDDING

This pudding snack with a crunch offers a healthy dose of omega-3s and probiotics that will help your little ones tummies.

Makes 3 servings

INGREDIENTS:

1½ cup plain kefir

2 tbsp honey

½ tsp vanilla extract

2 tbsp cocoa

2 tsp cinnamon

6 tbsp. chia seeds

DIRECTIONS:

1. In a blender or mixer combine all the ingredients except the chia seed.

2. To make this recipe work well everything needs to be evenly distributed. Chia seeds absorb liquid and you want the taste to be uniform.

3. Place mixture into a glass or plastic bowl. Stir well with a wooden spoon.

4. Stir in the chia seeds, making sure they are evenly distributed throughout the mixture.

5. Allow to set for 15 minutes then stir again. Repeat this process twice more.

6. Store in the refrigerator. This should keep for between three days to a week but you may need to add more kefir or milk to thin it out.

7. Pack in small jars or twist top containers if packing in a lunch.

8. Set next to an ice pack when in a lunch box.

CITRUS COOKIE CAKE

This lunchtime treat is a perfect balance between sweet and sour.

Makes 48 servings

INGREDIENTS:

2 packets shortbread cookies

1-15 oz can condensed milk

2 cups shredded coconut

4 oz butter, melted

Rind of 1 lemon, finely grated

2 cups powdered sugar

1 oz butter

3 tbsp lemon juice

DIRECTIONS:

1. Grease a large baking pan with butter and set aside.

2. In a blender or food processor, crush the cookies until they form decent sized crumbs.

3. Add coconut, lemon rind and condensed milk to the bowl and stir.

4. Add in butter and mix well. Then press into the prepared tin.

5. For the icing, combing the powdered sugar and remaining butter until combined.

6. Then add in lemon juice until the icing is smooth and easily spreadable.

7. Cover the coconut mixture with icing and refrigerate for 12 - 24 hours.

8. Cut and serve. If there is any left store in the refrigerator.

9. Place slices in individual containers with a lid before adding to the school lunch box.

10. Transport in an insulated box to keep the cookie cake fresh.

11. Remember to add a plastic teaspoon!

COCONUT OAT BARS

This easy recipe makes a sweet and chewy treat that your children will adore.

Makes 24 servings

INGREDIENTS:

1 cup rolled oats

½ cup brown or coconut sugar

¾ cup coconut

½ cup whole wheat flour (sifted)

½ cup self-rising flour (sifted)

5 oz butter

2 tbsp honey

¼ cup shredded coconut

DIRECTIONS:

1. Preheat oven to 350°F.

2. Line a baking pan with tin foil or parchment paper and grease with butter or non-stick spray.

3. Combined oats, sugar, coconut and flours in a large bowl and set aside.

4. In a saucepan, melt butter and honey until the mixture is well combined. This should take about 1 - 2 minutes with frequent stirring.

5. Remove from heat.

6. Make a well in the center of the dry ingredients and pour in the syrup.

7. Use a fork to combine, slowly mixing in the flour.

8. Mix until everything is moist and fully coated.

9. Press into the pan evenly and sprinkle with coconut.

10. Bake for 20 - 25 minutes.

11. Remove from the oven and sprinkle with more coconut

12. Leave to cool then cut into squares and serve.

13. These are easy to transport and just need to be wrapped on their own, before popping into the rest of the lunch for a crunchy treat.

CRANBERRY ORANGE BREAD

Perfect for breakfast or a snack, this versatile bread offers a touch of sweetness and tartness and may be served at any time of the day.

Makes 1 loaf

INGREDIENTS:

2 cups whole wheat flour

¼ cup sugar

1 tbsp baking power

½ tsp salt

1 orange rind, grated

$2/_3$ cup orange juice

2 eggs, lightly beaten

¼ cup unsweetened applesauce

¼ cup coconut oil, melted

1¼ cups fresh or frozen cranberries

½ cup chopped walnuts

DIRECTIONS:

1. Preheat oven to 350°F.

2. Line a loaf pan with tin foil and grease with non-stick spray then set aside.

3. In a medium bowl, sift in the dry ingredients then add in the orange rind and stir to mix.

4. Make a well in the dry ingredients and slowly add the wet ingredients.

5. Using a fork or spoon slowly incorporate the flour into the wet ingredients.

6. Do this slowly to make sure that it is properly mixed.

7. Slowly fold in the cranberries and walnuts.

8. Pour the batter into prepared pan and bake for 45 - 50 minutes or until an inserted knife comes out clean.

9. Leave to cool 10 minutes before slicing.

10. Add individual slices to the main lunch box for a sweet after lunch treat.

CREAMY LEMON SCONES

Here is a wonderful lunch or breakfast treat! Your family will flock to the table whenever you take them out of the oven.

Makes 12 servings

INGREDIENTS:

1 cup of lemonade

1 cup of heavy whipping cream

3 cups self-rising flour

1 egg, lightly beaten

DIRECTIONS:

1. Preheat oven to 450°F.

2. Line a cookie sheet with tin foil or parchment paper and spray with non-stick spray.

3. In a mixer, combine the ingredients except for the egg.

4. Mix until well combined and soft.

5. Place dough on a lightly floured surfaced and carefully press it down.

6. Do not do this hard and do not roll or the cookies will be too hard and tough.

7. Use a cookie cutter or drinking glass to cut circular pieces of dough.

8. Lay the cookies on the prepared cookie sheet and brush with the egg.

9. Cook for about ten minutes or until the tops are slightly browned.

10. Leave to cool slightly before serving.

11. Cut in half and butter. Wrap in plastic wrap before packing.

CRUNCHY CAKE

This delicious cake is a snap to make and a great alternative to unhealthy candy bars.

Makes 24 servings

INGREDIENTS:

Cake

10 oz packet of shortbread cookies

¾ cup chopped walnuts, pecans or almonds (or a mixture)

1 cup golden raisins

5 oz butter

5 ounces caster sugar

2 tbsp cocoa

2 tbsp coconut

1 tsp vanilla extract

1 egg, lightly beaten

Icing

1½ cups powdered sugar

2 tbsp cocoa

2 - 3 tbsp water

DIRECTIONS:

1. Line a large baking pan with tin foil and grease with butter or non-stick cooking spray.

2. Then, in a blender (or by hand) crush the cookies until they are crumbly. A fine powder is far too well crushed.

3. Place a small saucepan on medium heat.

4. Add in the butter, sugar and vanilla. Melt together stirring frequently.

5. Add in the biscuit mixture until well coated then add the egg.

6. If you want to be careful with potential bacteria, cook the mixture a while longer so as to avoid any egg borne pathogens.

7. Pour the mixture into the greased pan and spread evenly with a spoon.

8. To make the icing, combine the sugar and cocoa and then add enough water until it becomes an even, spreadable paste.

9. Spread over the top of the biscuit mixture and refrigerate for 12 - 24 hours.

10. Cut evenly and serve.

11. This cake will need to be kept cool in the lunch box and it would be best to place it in a separate container.

12. Use a freezer brick to keep cool and add a plastic spoon.

CUSTARD THUMBPRINT COOKIE

With a little bit of fruit flavor and a lot of sweetness, this is a wonderful cookie to include in a lunchbox.

Makes 24 cookies

INGREDIENTS:

Cookies

8 oz butter, at room temperature

1 cup brown or coconut sugar

2 tsp vanilla extract

2 cups self-rising flour

1 cup whole wheat flour

$2/3$ cup custard powder

$2/3$ cup shredded coconut

½ cup milk

Icing/filling

2 oz butter, softened

½ cup powdered sugar

¼ cup fruit jam

DIRECTIONS:

1. Preheat oven to 350°F.

2. Line a baking sheet with tinfoil and grease with non-stick spray.

3. In a mixer, cream together the sugar and butter until it is light and the sugar is not visually apparent.

4. Sift the flour and custard powder over the creamed sugar and then add in the coconut and mix well.

126

5. Roll out quarter sized pieces of dough and place them on the prepared pan.

6. Press your thumb into the center and drop a teaspoon sized amount of jam into the indentation.

7. Repeat with remaining dough.

8. Cook for 10 - 15 minutes or until golden brown.

9. Leave to cool.

10. To make the icing, mix the sugar and butter together in a saucepan over medium heat.

11. Stir to make sure that the sugar doesn't burn.

12. Drizzle over the tops of the cookies and leave to set.

13. Serve cool or store for up to a week.

14. These cookies can be wrapped a couple at a time and just popped into the lunch box for some extra energy.

DALMATIAN SCONES

Using two types of chocolate, these scones are a sweet treat sensation that is both easy to make and popular with the entire family.

Makes 15 scones

INGREDIENTS:

3 cups self-rising flour

2 tbsp baking powder

3 tbsp icing sugar

1 egg, lightly beaten

1½ cup milk

2 oz butter

½ package milk chocolate chips

½ package white chocolate chips

DIRECTIONS:

1. Preheat oven to 450°F.

2. Line a baking sheet with tinfoil and grease with either butter or non-stick cooking spray.

3. Into a mixing bowl, sift the flour, baking powder and sugar then stir in the liquid ingredients and chocolate chips.

4. Stir until just combined then placed on a lightly floured surface and leave for 20 minutes. Cover to stop the dough drying out.

5. Roll out to about 1" thickness and cut out circles using a round cookie cutter or an upside down drinking glass.

6. Place the circles on the prepared sheet and leave to rest for about 10 minutes.

7. Brush tops with milk and bake for 10 minutes or until slightly browned. Serve warm or cold.

8. Cold scones are suitable for the packed lunches.

9. Slice in half, butter and wrap in plastic wrap before putting in with the rest of the planned lunch.

EASY PANCAKE RECIPE

A much craved lunchbox surprise, pancakes are an old faithful that's sure to please. This basic recipe is easily customizable with fruit, spices and chocolate to suit everyone's taste.

Makes 8 Pancakes

INGREDIENTS:

1 cup whole wheat flour

½ tsp salt

1½ tsp baking soda

1 tbsp sugar

1 egg

¾ cup milk, buttermilk or kefir

2 oz butter, melted

Fruit, chocolate chips, cinnamon (optional)

DIRECTIONS:

1. In a small bowl, mix the flour, salt, baking soda and sugar together.

2. Whisk in the egg and milk a little at a time until the batter is smooth. Add cinnamon or fold in fruit or chocolate chips.

3. Heat a small griddle or frying man and grease with butter.

4. In ¼ cup portions, pour in the batter.

5. Cook until the top bubbles and the edges seem solid then flip and cook the other side. Both sides should be golden brown.

6. Serve immediately or cool and freeze in small portions.

7. These will keep for about month and can be reheated in the microwave.

8. For a school lunch box, defrost if frozen and spread each with some hazelnut spread or strawberry jam before rolling up.

9. Wrap the rolls separately or in pairs and place in a separate container.

10. Add to the main lunch box as an extra special treat.

FLOUR-LESS PEANUT BUTTER COOKIES

These gluten free cookies are a delicious treat that children and adults of all ages will enjoy.

Makes 12 cookies

INGREDIENTS:

1 cup peanut butter

½ cup caster sugar

1 egg

DIRECTIONS:

1. Pre-heat oven to 350°F.

2. Line a baking tray with foil or parchment paper and grease with non-stick spray.

3. Mix together ingredients in a bowl or mixer until well combined.

4. Take tablespoons of the mixture and place on the tray.

5. Flatten with a fork or flat bottomed drinking glass.

6. Bake for 10 - 15 minutes and then leave until cool on a paper towel.

7. Serve warm or store in plastic container for up to a week.

8. Send a couple of these wrapped separately for lunch – add to the main lunch box.

FRUIT AND NUT BARS

Commercial fruit and nut bars are often loaded with unnecessary amounts of fillers and sugar. This recipe is a healthy substitute for those processed treats and your kids will like them just as much.

Makes 24 small bars

INGREDIENTS:

¼ cup dried apricots, chopped

¼ cup dried dates, chopped

¼ cup dried apples, chopped

2 cups whole wheat flour

2 tsp baking powder

2 eggs

¾ cups brown or coconut sugar

1 tsp ground cinnamon

1 tsp vanilla

¼ tsp salt

½ cup chopped pecans

DIRECTIONS:

1. Preheat oven to 350°F. Line a baking pan with tinfoil or parchment paper and grease with butter or non-stick spray

2. Submerge the dried fruit in boiling water and leave for 5 minutes before draining and allowing them to cool.

3. Combine the dry ingredients in a bowl and mix in the wet ingredients and pecans.

4. Spoon into the tin and flatten with the back of a spoon.

5. Bake for 30 minutes and cut while still warm.

6. When cold, wrap and add to your child's lunch especially if they have a long day with sport after school – these will give them an extra, all important energy boost.

FRUITY BUTTERMILK MUFFINS

Good for breakfast or an afternoon snack, these muffins offer the dual flavors of sweet and tart. Perfect for kids who need something healthy, but want something sweet.

Makes 12 muffins

INGREDIENTS:

2½ cups white whole wheat flour

½ tsp salt

3 tsp baking powder

¼ cup brown sugar, coconut sugar or caster sugar

½ tsp cinnamon

$1^1/_3$ cups buttermilk

¼ cup olive oil or coconut oil

1 egg

7 oz frozen mixed berries

1 small mango or peach, peeled and sliced

DIRECTIONS:

1. Preheat oven to 375°F and fill a muffin tin with 12 paper cupcake/muffin liners. If using tin foil liners consider lightly greasing.

2. In a small bowl combine the flour, cinnamon, salt, baking powder and sugar; set aside.

3. In another bowl, whisk together the buttermilk, oil and egg until fully combined then slowly stir into flour mixture.

4. Do not over stir. At this point the mixture should still be lumpy and the flour and liquid just barely combined.

5. Gently fold in berries, careful not to break them.

6. Spoon the mixture into muffin pans, leaving half an inch of head space at the top so that the muffins do not overflow.

7. Top with mango or peach slices.

8. Bake for 25 minutes or until a knife inserted into the muffins comes out clean.

9. Remove muffins from tin and leave to cool.

10. Serve immediately or wrap individually and freeze for up to a month.

11. Take straight from the freezer! What could be easier?

12. Add to the lunch box and when eating time arrives the muffins will have defrosted. Voila!

HAZELNUT SPIRALS

Crunchy and sweet, these twists are a light and delicious treat for all year round.

Makes 10 twists

INGREDIENTS:

2 sheets frozen puff pastry, thawed

½ cup chocolate hazelnut spread

Beaten egg

Finely chopped hazel nuts

DIRECTIONS:

1. Preheat oven to 350°F.

2. Line a baking sheet with tinfoil or parchment paper and spray with non-stick spray.

3. Lay the pastry sheets on the counter and smear the hazelnut spread on both sheets.

4. Press the two sheets together carefully and cut into strips.

5. If some of the nut spread leaks out just wipe it away

6. Take each strip and twist until it is gently spiraled.

7. Lay on the prepared baking sheet. Repeat with the remaining dough.

8. Brush the pastry twists with beaten egg and sprinkle with the chopped nuts.

9. Cook for 10 - 15 minutes until the dough is puffed up, crisp and golden.

10. Cool and serve.

11. These are easily broken so place a few in a separate container to send to school.

HOMEMADE GRANOLA BARS

Granola bars are an easily transportable snack but with all the extra sugar and preservatives in them they aren't always the healthiest snack. This recipe is a healthy, simple one you'll feel good giving to your kids and they'll love eating.

Makes 24 servings

INGREDIENTS:

½ cup honey

5 oz butter

2 cups crushed cornflakes

2 cups rice krispies

1 cup raisins

½ cup flax seeds

½ cup chopped apricots, dates, semi-sweet chocolate chips or a mix of the three

½ cup shredded coconut (unsweetened preferred

½ cup pumpkin seeds, sunflower seeds, sesame seeds or a mix of the three.

DIRECTIONS:

1. Preheat oven to 350°F.

2. Line a large baking pan with foil or parchment paper and grease with butter or non-stick spray.

3. In a medium sauce pan over medium heat, combine honey and butter.

4. Stir frequently to prevent scalding. Cook for 2 - 3 minutes. Butter should be melted and the honey should be less thick.

5. Bring to a boil, stirring frequently, until the syrup thickens. Immediately remove from heat.

6. In a large bowl, mix the remaining ingredients well then pour in the syrup and stir.

7. Be careful as the syrup will be exceedingly hot. If your children are helping you cook make sure they are a distance away.

8. Once the dry ingredients are coated with the syrup begin to spoon it into the prepared pan.

9. You can use wet fingers to smooth out the top but this is not necessary.

10. Bake for 15 - 20 minutes or until slightly brown.

11. Refrigerate for 12 - 24 hours and then cut.

12. Serve.

13. Wrap each bar individually for taking to school.

14. Just pop into the main lunch box!

JAM BUNDLES

These fruity little bundles are extremely versatile. Low in unnecessary sugar they are a perfect snack for lunch, a wonderful after dinner treat or even a great replacement for pop-tarts at breakfast.

Makes 9 servings

INGREDIENTS:

1 puff pastry sheet, thawed

¼ cup cream cheese

¼ cup no sugar added jam

Cinnamon (optional)

Brown or coconut sugar (optional)

DIRECTIONS:

1. In a small bowl, combine cream cheese and jam, mixing until properly combined. Set aside.

2. Lay out puff pastry sheet and, using a knife or pizza cutter, slice into 9 equal sized pieces.

3. Using a small spoon put approximately 2 - 3 tablespoons of filling into the center of a piece of puff pastry.

4. Take two of the corners that are diagonal from each other and press together.

5. If they do not stick, trace some water around the edge and try again. Then pull the other two corners up and pressed together.

6. Pinch along the seams to close and place on a greased baking sheet.

7. Repeat with remaining puff pastry squares and filling.

8. Sprinkle with cinnamon and sugar.

9. At this point, you can freeze the bundles if you like. They keep for up to a month in the freezer.

10. If you wish cook them, heat the oven to 400°F and bake them for 15 minutes or until slightly browned and crispy.

11. Leave to cool and then serve.

12. Only sent the cooked parcels as part of the lunch menu!

13. Wrap carefully as the pastry may crumble and pack separately for the best results.

KEFIR BLUEBERRY MUFFINS

Kefir is a probiotic milk drink with a host of health benefits. It gives this muffin an interesting tang to compliment the sweetness of the blueberry.

Makes 18 muffins

INGREDIENTS:

½ cup (approximately two sticks) butter

2 eggs

¾ cup plain kefir

1 cup all-purpose flour, sifted

1 cup whole wheat flour, sifted

¼ cup brown or coconut sugar

1 tbsp baking powder

2 cups frozen or fresh blueberries

DIRECTIONS:

1. Preheat oven to 350°F and coat a muffin pan with non-stick spray. If desired you can use cupcake or muffin liners but this is not necessary.

2. In a large bowl or mixer cream together the eggs, butter and sugar until blended.

3. Add in kefir and blend.

4. Once it is sufficiently mixed, slowly add in the dry ingredients.

5. Carefully fold in the blueberries. Be mindful not to break them or you will end up with overly gooey or blue muffins

6. Spoon mixture evenly into the muffin pan and put into the oven.

7. Bake for 15 - 20 minutes or until an inserted knife comes out clean.

8. Keep in mind that this recipe has berries in it so if your knife comes out blue, wipe it off and try another muffin.

9. You are looking for dough on the knife, not blueberry.

10. Cool before serving.

11. These muffins can be frozen in individual bags for up to two weeks.

12. What could be easier?

13. Straight from the freezer in the morning, defrosted and delicious by recess and the lunch bell.

LEMON CHEESECAKE DESSERT BARS

Tangy and chewy with a hint of sweetness, this is the perfect snack to add to any lunchbox. Your kids will love it and you'll find it convenient to make - a blessing on those busy weekdays.

Makes 12

INGREDIENTS:

2 packets Lattice Biscuits

8oz unsalted butter

1 cup caster sugar

1 cup cream cheese spread

1 packet unflavored gelatin

$1/_3$ cup lemon juice (fresh or bottled)

DIRECTIONS:

1. In a mixer, cream together the butter, sugar and cream cheese until fluffy and light colored.

2. Using the microwave, heat the lemon juice then add the gelatin and stir.

3. Quickly, before it has the chance to cool, pour into the sugar mixture and turn the mixer on low.

4. Continue to mix until it is completely smooth.

5. Line a baking pan with tin foil and spray it with non-stick spray.

6. In the bottom of the pan, lay out a layer of lattice biscuits.

7. Pour the cream over the top than lay another layer of lattice cookies on top of that.

8. Refrigerate until the gelatin has set, approximately 12 hours.

9. Cut into squares or slices and serve.

10. These will need to be kept cool in the lunch box and should be packed in a separate container.

11. Add a freezer brick for cooling and a teaspoon to eat this delicious dessert.

LOVELY LEMON PASTRY

This slightly tart cake will be a hit with your family, sure to delight young and old.

Makes 12 servings

INGREDIENTS:

Cake

5 oz unsalted butter

1 cup caster sugar

1 tbsp finely chopped lemon rind

3 eggs

2 cups flour

2 tsp baking powder

$1/_3$ cup lemon juice

1 cup milk or kefir

Icing

1½ cups powdered sugar

1 - 2 tbsp lemon juice

DIRECTIONS:

1. Preheat oven to 350°F.

2. Line a round cake pan with tinfoil and grease well with butter to prevent sticking.

3. In a mixer cream together the butter, sugar and lemon rind in light colored and fluffy. Sugar should not be visibly apparent.

4. At this point add in the eggs and continue to mix well.

5. Once the eggs are fully incorporated, add in the flour and baking powder, ½ cup at a time; then pour in the milk and lemon juice.

6. Continue to mix on a low speed until the batter is combined and smooth.

7. Pour the mixture into prepared pan and bake for 50 minutes or until an inserted knife comes out clean.

8. Make the icing while the cake is cooling by whisking together the powdered sugar and lemon until it's become a smooth, easily spreadable paste.

9. Once the cake is completely cool, spread the icing over the top of the cake.

10. Do not be surprised if it make a bit of a mess, this is fine. It adds to the appearance!

11. Allow it to set first before serving. This will take about 30 minutes.

12. Wrap individual slices in plastic wrap or place in a separate container with a lid.

13. Add to the planned lunch box for a special Friday treat!

NEWSPAPER CAKE

A creatively colored treat, this will be something both you and your children will love having as an afternoon snack.

Makes 10-12 servings

INGREDIENTS:

8 oz butter, softened

1 cup caster sugar

1 tsp vanilla

2 eggs

2 cups self-rising flour

½ cup plus 1 tbsp milk

Red Food coloring

2 tbsp cocoa powder

2 tbsp butter, softened

1 cup icing sugar

1 tbsp cocoa powder

1-2 tbsp milk

DIRECTIONS:

1. Preheat oven to 350°F.

2. Line an 8" cake with tin foil and grease with either butter or non-stick cooking spray.

3. Cream together the sugar and butter in an electric mixer until it is creamy and the sugar is not visibly apparent.

4. Add in the vanilla, continuing to mix, then add in the eggs one at a time until the batter is smooth.

5. In half-cup portions, add in the flour then the milk and continue to mix.

6. Pour equal amounts of batter into three separate bowls.

7. Set one bowl aside. To one of the others add the cocoa powder and a tablespoon of milk and mix until completely combined.

8. In the final dish add the red food coloring until the batter is a deep bread.

9. With three different spoons, alternately drop spoonfuls of the different colored batters into the pan until full.

10. Run a skewer or knife through the batter a couple of times before placing in the oven to cook for 30 - 40 minutes or until an inserted knife comes out clean.

11. Leave to cool before icing.

12. To make the icing, combine the ingredients in a bowl and mix until smooth. An electric hand mixer is very useful for this.

13. Spread over the cake when cool.

14. Slices can be individually wrapped and added to the lunch box.

15. So delicious that it won't make it to the afternoon to be eaten!

NUT BUTTER JELLY POCKETS

Portable, and less messy nut butter and jelly was a wonderful invention. Here's a homemade and healthy, quick to make lunch for those hectic mornings.

Makes 6 servings

INGREDIENTS:

12 pieces of whole wheat bread

Nut butter (peanut butter, almond butter, sesame seed butter, etc.)

Fruit jelly or jam

DIRECTIONS:

1. Lay out the twelve pieces of bread on the counter.

2. On six of them spread your nut butter and on the other six spread your jam.

3. Make sure to leave space around the edges. Lay the peanut butter covered slices evenly over the jelly ones.

4. With either a sandwich sealer (generally sold at most supermarkets) or a large drinking glass, press down firmly for 30 seconds.

5. Then cut around the glass and remove. This should leave you with a nice, neat pocket.

6. These can be served immediately or frozen.

7. If frozen, they can simply be put in a lunch box and allowed to thaw naturally.

HAZELNUT OATMEAL PIE

This recipe takes the amazing flavor of chocolate hazelnut spread and adds a creative twist to a family favorite.

Serves 6

INGREDIENTS:

3 cups whole wheat flour

3 cups rolled oats

1¼ cups brown or coconut sugar

1½ tsp baking powder

½ tsp salt

13 oz butter, melted

20 oz hazelnut spread

DIRECTIONS:

1. Preheat oven to 350°F.

2. Line a 9"x12" baking pan with foil or parchment paper and grease with non-stick spray.

3. Combine the dry ingredients in a small bowl and stir until evenly mixed.

4. Pour in the butter and combine until the dry ingredients are thoroughly coated and incorporated. If you see any dry spots continue to stir.

5. Press all but 2 cups of the oat batter into the prepared pan.

6. In the microwave, melt the hazelnut spread until it is easily pourable.

7. This should only take about a minute so keep your eye on it.

8. Pour this over the oat mixture than cover it with the remaining 2 cups.

9. Bake for 25 minutes then leave to cool in the refrigerator for 12 - 24 hours.

10. Cut into squares and serve.

11. Lots of energy here and great added as a pudding to the lunch box. Wrap the squares individually or place in a separate small container.

NUTTY POUND CAKE

With a fruity glaze, this twist on an old classic is perfect alongside any lunch.

Makes 6-8 servings

INGREDIENTS:

½ cup almond meal

1 cup whole wheat flour, sifted

2 tsp baking powder

1 cup caster sugar

Zest of one orange, finely grated

¾ cup Greek yogurt

3 eggs, lightly beaten

¼ cup sunflower oil

¼ cup orange marmalade

DIRECTIONS:

1. Preheat oven to 350°C.

2. Put foil in a loaf pan and grease with non-stick pan. Or, if you would like, grease a small Bundt pan.

3. In a large mixing bowl or mixer, combine the almond meal, flour and baking soda.

4. In a separate bowl, combine the sugar and zest until they are aromatic. It should be easily detectable from a slight distance.

5. Add the yogurt and eggs, whisking until well incorporated.

6. Pour the wet ingredients into the dry and mix thoroughly by hand or with the mixer.

7. Carefully fold in sunflower oil and then pour into the greased pan.

8. Bake for 35 minutes or until an inserted knife comes out clean.

9. Alternately, remove when the cake is pulling away from the sides of the pan and is golden on top.

10. Leave to cool until just slightly warm.

11. Combine the marmalade and 1 tablespoon of water.

12. Brush the mixture over the top of the cake and allow it to cool.

13. Serve.

14. Add individual slices to your child's lunch. Wrap and pop one in!

POLKA DOT FRUIT CAKE

Sometimes fruit cake is hard and sticky. But this cake is different.
Succulent with just the right amount of sweetness, it is easy to cook and
easy to pack for a lunchtime snack.

Makes 1 cake

INGREDIENTS:

17 oz golden raisins

8 oz unsalted butter, softened

1 cup caster sugar

4 eggs

3 cups self-rising flour

DIRECTIONS:

1. Preheat oven to 300°F.

2. Line an 8" cake pan with foil and grease with butter. Set aside

3. Cook the raisins in boiling water for approximately 10 minutes, drain and add the butter into the pan.

4. Cover and cook on low, allowing the butter to melt.

5. In a mixer, beat the eggs and sugar together until completely mixed and smooth.

6. In a separate bowl add the flour and pour the egg mixture into it, mixing until the batter is smooth.

7. Add in the butter/raisin mixture and gently stir to mix. This will make the dots so stir well.

8. Pour that into the cake pan and cook for approximately an hour and a half or until an inserted knife comes out clean.

9. Remove from oven and leave to cool before serving.

10. Slices must be wrapped before adding to the basic lunch box.

QUICK BAKE GINGER COOKIES

Really quick to make with ultimate crunch!

Makes 30 cookies

INGREDIENTS:

$^2/_3$ cup vegetable oil

1½ cups light brown sugar

1 large egg

4 tbsp. treacle

2 cups sifted whole wheat flour

2 tsp baking soda

1¼ tsp ground cinnamon

1¼ tsp ground ginger

¼ tsp salt

DIRECTIONS:

11. Preheat oven to 350°F.

12. Mix the vegetable oil and 1 cup of the sugar in a large bowl.

13. Beat in the egg really well.

14. Stir in the treacle.

15. Sift in the flour, baking soda and spices and stir until it just comes together.

16. Put the rest of the sugar in a spate bowl.

17. Roll the dough into 1 inch balls and roll each one in the sugar.

18. Place far apart on ungreased baking sheets. Do not flatten.

19. Bake until set but still soft, 10 – 12 minutes.

20. Transfer to a wire rack to cool. Store in an airtight container.

21. Place a couple of these in a separate container and add to the main lunch – yum!

RASPBERRY CHIA CRUMBLE

With all the benefits of omega-3's and fiber, this crumble is a nutritional power house. But it tastes so good your family won't realize they're eating healthily!

Makes 16 slices

INGREDIENTS:

2 cups raspberries, chopped

½ cup water

¼ cup coconut sugar

½ lemon, juiced

½ tsp vanilla extract

½ tsp ginger powder

¼ cup chia seeds

¼ cup dried goji berries (optional)

1 cup almond meal

1 cup brown rice flour

2 large apples, chopped and pureed

¼ cup coconut sugar

½ cup rolled oats

½ cup shredded coconut

DIRECTIONS:

1. Preheat oven to 350°F.

2. Grease a glass casserole pan and set aside.

3. Heat a saucepan over medium-low heat and add the berries, water, sugar, lemon juice, vanilla and ginger then cook for 10 minutes or until the berries are able to be easily mashed.

4. Remove from the heat.

5. To this mixture, add the chia seeds and goji berries. It will thicken up so don't try to hurry the process.

6. If it turns out too runny add more chia seeds in tablespoon sized amounts until thicker.

7. In a mixing bowl, combine the flours, coconut, apple puree and sugar and mix until it is crumbly.

8. Spoon two-thirds of the flour mixture into the prepared dish and press into a crust.

9. Then cook for 12 - 15 minutes.

10. Stir the oats into the remaining flour mixture and set aside.

11. Once the crust has browned, remove from the oven and pour the chia seed mixture over it.

12. Add the oat topping and bake for an additional 20 - 25 minutes.

13. Leave to cool before slicing.

14. Put separate pieces in containers to add to the lunches. This is necessary as the 'oaty' bits will find themselves over everything else!

15. If soft add a plastics spoon to eat.

16. It would be best to send this in an insulated container to keep it cool.

SEEDED FRUIT COOKIE

Kids love sweets but it is sometimes hard to balance out health with taste. This cookie does all of that. Offering a generous helping of fiber and fruit, these are cookies that kids will love and you'll feel good giving them.

Makes 20 pieces

INGREDIENTS:

4 oz unsalted butter

¼ cup brown sugar or coconut sugar

2 tbsp honey

3 tbsp water

1 tsp baking soda

1 cup rolled oats

½ cup cooked quinoa

1 cup whole wheat flour

¼ cup sesame seeds

3 tbsp ground flaxseed

$^2/_3$ cup chopped dried apricots

$^2/_3$ cup dried cranberries.

DIRECTIONS:

1. Preheat oven to 350°F.

2. Line two baking trays with foil or parchment paper and grease with either butter or non-stick spray.

3. In a medium saucepan, combine butter, sugar, honey and water and cook over medium heat, stirring frequently.

4. Honey and Sugar can burn even at lower temperatures so be vigilant.

5. Heat the mixture until the butter melts and is smoothly incorporated with the other ingredients.

6. Remove from heat, stir in the baking soda and set aside.

7. In another bowl, combine the oats, quinoa, flour, sesame seeds and flax seeds.

8. Add in the butter mixture and fruit, stirring until well combined.

9. This will be a slightly crumbly recipe do don't be surprised when it does not appear like typical cookie dough

10. Rolls tablespoon size balls of the dough and place 2 inches apart on the baking trays.

11. Use a fork to flatten.

12. Bake for 8 minutes or until slightly browned.

13. Remove from oven and leave to cool slightly before transferring to a wire rack or paper towels.

14. Can be served warm or completely cooled.

15. This is best stored in a plastic container and will last up to 5 days.

16. Easy cookies to add at the last minute to the main lunch goodies.

17. Wrap in pairs and just put them in!

SIMPLE JUICE CAKE

Sweetened naturally, this cake is far healthier than the majority of cake mixes available and just as easy. It tastes so good that your kids will be begging you to make more to send with them to school.

Makes 1 cake

INGREDIENTS:

35 oz mixed dried fruits

2½ cups fruit juice of choice

2 cups self-rising flour

DIRECTIONS:

1. Preheat oven to 350°F.

2. Line a cake pan with tinfoil and grease with either non-stick cooking spray or butter

3. In a small pot or saucepan combine the dried fruit and 2 cups of the fruit juice.

4. Bring to a boil then quickly reduce the heat and simmer on low for 3 minutes.

5. Remove from the heat and leave to cool for 2 hours, uncovered.

6. This will make a type of watery syrup to put into the cake.

7. Once cooled, sift the flour into the pot until well mixed.

8. Add in the last bit of juice to make the batter thinner and more easy use.

9. Pour it into the prepared pan and bake for two hours or until a knife inserted into the center comes out clean.

10. Cool completely before slicing and adding to a lunch box.

SOUR FRUIT SALAD

Good to pack as a side treat; this salad balances out the added sugar with fresh fruit. If your little ones are picky about the healthy food they eat, try this recipe.

Makes 10-12 servings

INGREDIENTS:

1-20 oz can pineapple chunks, drained

1-15 oz can fruit cocktail, drained

1-15 oz can mandarin oranges, drained

1 cup sour cream

2½ cups whipped topping

3 cups mini marshmallows

DIRECTIONS:

1. Combine the fruits in a small bowl, stirring to mix them all together.

2. In another bowl, whip together the sour cream and whipped topping until they are completely mixed.

3. Fold the fruit and marshmallows into the cream mixture, careful not to break the fruit apart or tear the marshmallows.

4. Serve cold.

5. If you are packing this in a lunchbox, pour a serving into a small plastic container with a tight lid and sit next to a cold pack.

6. Remember to add a plastic teaspoon!

STAINED GLASS COOKIE

Perfect for any holiday or rainy day, these cookies are both delicious and fascinating for little kitchen helpers.

Makes 36 cookies

INGREDIENTS:

6 oz butter

¾ cup brown or coconut sugar

1 egg

1 tsp vanilla extract

¾ tsp salt

1½ cup white whole wheat flour, sifted

1 cup all-purpose flour

6 - 8 oz fruit flavored candies broken up and separated by color

DIRECTIONS:

1. Preheat oven to 350°F.

2. Line a cookie sheet(s) with tinfoil and grease with non-stick cooking spray.

3. In a mixer, cream together the butter and sugar until fluffy and slightly colored. The sugar should not be easily visible.

4. This process should take about 2 or 3 minutes

5. Add in the egg, salt and vanilla.

6. Lower the speed of the mixer and add in the flour slowly, ½ a cup at a time, until it is all completely combined.

7. Turn out the dough on a lightly floured surface and roll into a thin rectangle.

8. $1/8$" thickness is preferred however ¼" can be used.

9. This part could be fun for the kids. Choose large circular cookie cutters and cut out the shapes from the dough.

10. Then, using another cookie cutter that is half the size of the original one, cut out the center of the circles.

11. Repeat process with remaining dough

12. Sprinkle approximate 1 - 2 tsp (depending on cut out size) into the cut out in the cookies. Keep the colors separate to prevent bleeding.

13. Cook for 7 - 9 minutes or until the edges are golden brown.

14. Remove from oven and allow to completely cool.

15. Do not attempt to take them off of the baking sheet until cool because the cookies break.

16. To add to a lunch box it would be best to put these in a small rigid container to prevent a crumb treat instead of a biscuit treat!

SUCCULENT CARROT CAKE WITH CREAM CHEESE ICING

Carrot cake is a healthy and enjoyable treat that any kid can enjoy. The added coconut oil adds certain richness to a popular recipe.

Makes 8 servings

INGREDIENTS:

CAKE

1 cup white whole wheat flour

¾ tsp baking soda

1 tsp baking powder

½ tsp cinnamon

½ tsp nutmeg

½ tsp salt

2 eggs

¾ cup brown or coconut sugar

½ cup melted coconut oil

7 oz can crush pineapple, drained

1 cup grated carrot

$1/_3$ cup chopped walnuts

ICING

¼ cup cream cheese

¼ cup powdered sugar

½ tsp. vanilla extract

DIRECTIONS:

1. Preheat oven to 350°F.

2. Line a cake pan with parchment paper or tinfoil, then grease with butter or nonstick spray.

3. Combine all cake ingredients save for the carrots, pineapple and walnuts.

4. Once mixed, carefully fold in remaining ingredients.

5. Pour into the pan and bake for 45 - 50 minutes or until an inserted knife comes out clean.

6. While the house begins to smell like spices, begin to make the icing.

7. For the icing, combine ingredients in a small bowl and beat together using a whisk or electric beater.

8. Remove cooked cake and leave to cool on wire rack.

9. Spread the frosting over the top and cut into 8 pieces.

10. If preferred this cake can be left un-iced for lunch box addition as it will be easier for the youngsters to handle.

11. Wrap each slice individually and add to the main goodies.

SWEET CREAM CHEESE SANDWICH

This recipe is simple but flavorful. It blends the unique taste of cream cheese with the sweetness of dried fruit and the softness of the bread with the crunch of the celery. It is a perfect warm weather meal on its own or a good accompaniment to soup during the cold months.

Makes 1 serving

INGREDIENTS:

2 slices whole wheat or multigrain bread

1½ tbsp spreadable cream cheese

½ carrot, coarsely grated

1 tbsp golden raisins

1 tbsp dried cranberries

Celery, finely chopped

Baby spinach leaves

DIRECTIONS:

1. Spread the cream cheese on the bread in a thin layer.

2. Cover cream cheese with carrots, fruit, celery and baby spinach.

3. Top with the second slice of bread and slice diagonally through the center.

4. This sweet sandwich could be a dessert or a main course in a lunch box.

5. You will need to wrap it well in plastic wrap and place in an insulated lunch box to keep it cool and fresh.

SWEET NUT BUTTER BALLS

A wonderful sweet treat, these little balls are a quick no-bake cookie that will more than likely be eaten before they have the chance to make it to the lunch boxes. It's also a fun recipe to get your younger ones involved in the kitchen.

Makes 16 servings

INGREDIENTS:

2 cups crushed graham crackers

½ cup brown or coconut sugar

2 cups peanut butter or almond butter

¼ cup butter

½ cups raisins, chopped

DIRECTIONS:

1. In a mixing bowl or blender, combine the sugar, nut butter, butter and raisins and mix together until it forms thick dough.

2. Drop out on to a wax paper covered surface.

3. Place graham crackers in a bowl.

4. Take two tablespoons of dough and roll it into a ball.

5. Place the ball into the graham cracker powder and roll to coat.

6. This is a perfect job for little hands!

7. Keep in the refrigerator for up to a week.

8. Pack in small container to send along in a lunchbox.

SWEET OATMEAL BALLS

Oatmeal is healthy meal but sometimes hard to send in a lunch box. These oatmeal balls offer all the filling health benefits of that popular food without the typical mess.

Makes 20

INGREDIENTS:

¾ cup oatmeal

¼ cup flaxseeds

1 tbsp honey

1 tbsp peanut or almond butter

¼ cup raisins

1 - 2 tbsp milk

½ cup desiccated coconut

DIRECTIONS:

1. Using a food processor or blender, process the oatmeal, flaxseeds and raisins for roughly 30 seconds.

2. To the oatmeal mixture, add the honey and peanut butter and process for another 30 seconds.

3. At this point, attempt to make a ball out of the batter.

4. If it falls apart, add the milk a tablespoon at a time and process until you are able to roll it into a cohesive ball.

5. Then roll in the coconut.

6. Serve immediately or place in an airtight container and store.

7. Pop into a small container or wrap separately before sending off to school for a special sweet treat.

TRAIL MIX BREAKFAST BARS

These bars offer a blast of nutrition and are a quick fix for the harried morning round up. While they are a 'breakfast' bar they work just as well for a midday snack that your little ones will love.

Makes 18 pieces

INGREDIENTS:

¾ cup whole wheat flour

1½ tsp baking powder

1 tsp salt

1 cup shredded coconut (preferably unsweetened)

¼ cup brown sugar or coconut sugar

½ cup pumpkin seeds

½ cup sunflower seeds

$1/3$ cup golden raisins

¼ cup cranberries

$1/3$ cup chopped dried apricots

¼ cup flax seeds

¾ cup milk

1 egg

DIRECTIONS:

1. Preheat the oven to 350°F.

2. Line a 13 x 9 baking pan with parchment paper or tinfoil and grease with either butter or non-stick spray.

3. In a bowl, combine fruits, seeds and dry ingredients and set aside.

4. In another bowl, whisk together the wet ingredients until fully combined.

5. Add the wet ingredients to the dry and mix until fully incorporated.

6. This will be a thick mixture and should look a little bit like very wet trail mix.

7. If it is too wet or too dry add flour or milk as needed.

8. Spoon the mixture into the pan and spread it out edge to edge.

9. If the top is not smooth, shake and tap the pan until the mixture evens out.

10. Bake for 30 minutes or until firm.

11. Remove from oven and leave to cool on a wire rack.

12. Slice and serve.

13. These bars may also be refrigerated for up to a week.

14. Wrap separately from the main lunchtime lunch box meal and add to the same box or as a separate item, whichever you prefer!

ZUCCHINI WALNUT BREAD

Squash is an extremely healthy food to incorporate into your kid's diet. This sweet bread offers all the nutrition of zucchini with a taste that your little ones will love.

Makes 8 servings

INGREDIENTS:

1¾ cups white whole wheat flour

1 tsp cinnamon

½ tsp salt

2½ tsp baking powder

½ cup milk

½ cup brown sugar

2 eggs

4 oz butter, melted

1 cup grated zucchini

½ cup walnuts

DIRECTIONS:

1. Preheat oven to 350°F.

2. Line a bread pan with tinfoil or parchment paper and grease with butter or non-stick spray.

3. In a small bowl, sift together flour, cinnamon, salt and baking powder.

4. Slowly add in the rest of the ingredients except for the butter.

5. Mix it together until well combined.

6. Finally, add in the melted butter.

7. Carefully pour into the bread pan and bake for 45 minutes or until the knife comes out clean.

8. Remove from pan and leave to cool before slicing.

9. Serve immediately or freeze into individuals slices.

10. If packing in a lunchbox, allow to thaw in the refrigerator overnight or place a frozen slice directly into the lunch box.

11. It will defrost well before lunch time.

THANK YOU

If you and your kids enjoyed this, and I'm guessing their taste buds did, please keep an out for some of the other fun recipe books I've created!

Thanks so much to my family, my friends, and most of all my kids for being such amazing and willing taste testers, helping me in the kitchen and making me laugh every day.

Be good to each other!

Naomi Potter

87414053R00115

Made in the USA
San Bernardino, CA
04 September 2018